FLAGSHIPS OF TH

FLAGSHIPS OF THE SPIRIT
Cathedrals in Society

EDITED BY

STEPHEN PLATTEN
&
CHRISTOPHER LEWIS

DARTON · LONGMAN + TODD

First published in 1998 by
Darton, Longman and Todd Ltd
1 Spencer Court
140–142 Wandsworth High Street
London SW18 4JJ

ISBN 0–232–52197–2

A catalogue record for this book is available
from the British Library.

Designed by Sandie Boccacci
Phototypeset in 11/14pt Aldus
by Intype London Ltd
Printed and bound in Great Britain
by Redwood Books, Trowbridge, Wiltshire

CONTENTS

❧

v

CONTENTS

LIST OF ILLUSTRATIONS

THE CONTRIBUTORS

NICOLAS ALLDRIT taught theology at Lincoln Theological College and is now Rector of the Witham group of parishes in the Diocese of Lincoln.

ANDREW ANDERSON is Surveyor to St Albans Cathedral.

SUSAN HILL has been a professional novelist, playwright and critic since 1963.

CHRISTOPHER LEWIS is Dean of St Albans Cathedral. He has also worked at Canterbury Cathedral, been a parish priest and taught theology.

STEPHEN PLATTEN teaches and writes theology. He is Dean of Norwich and sometime Canon Residentiary of Portsmouth Cathedral.

CHRISTOPHER ROWLAND is Dean Ireland Professor of the Exegesis of Holy Scripture at Oxford University. Before that he was for twelve years Dean of Chapel at Jesus College Cambridge. He has written on the apocalyptic tradition in Judaism and Christianity and on Latin American Liberation Theology.

RICHARD SHEPHARD is Head Master at the Minster School, York. He is Sub-Chamberlain of York Minster and Honorary Visiting Fellow of the Department of Music at York University.

DAVID STANCLIFFE is Bishop of Salisbury and Chairman of the Liturgical Commission. Previously he was Provost of Portsmouth during the period when Portsmouth Cathedral was completed and reordered.

ANGELA TILBY is a tutor at Westcott House theological college in Cambridge and is also a freelance broadcaster and television producer.

KEITH WALKER is Canon Librarian at Winchester Cathedral. He is responsible for numerous church commissions of visual art and is author of *Images and Idols*.

INTRODUCTION

Images conjure up in people's minds wildly varying pictures and associations. Indeed, part of the significance of an image is to bring together in the mind of the reader or observer concepts and ideas that might never before have been associated with each other. This is part of the process of the human imagination which seeks new patterns of thought and contributes to the enrichment of culture. A phrase like 'flagships of the spirit' doubtless does all this. It brings with it both negative and positive allusions. What springs to mind at the mention of a flagship? It may be Nelson, standing on the deck of HMS *Victory*, rallying his troops before battle with the immortal words: 'England expects that every man will do his duty'. A more recent image might be of HMS *Hermes* steaming down into southern latitudes leading the task force into the Falklands conflict.

The more obviously negative and militaristic tones of the word 'flagship' are evident – though we would hardly wish our cathedrals to be seen as instruments of aggressive spiritual warfare. Furthermore, some of the allusions that gather around 'flagship' may feel too triumphalistic and pompous to be associated with contemporary views either of the Church generally, or of cathedrals in particular. Alongside these negative associations, however, lie more subtle allusions. HMS *Victory* was symbolic of Horatio Nelson's leadership, and its focal place within the fleet was a fillip to morale. Even *Hermes*, during the Falklands War, communicated a symbolic message which was positive and encouraging to all whose duty it was to fight (despite controversy that still rages over the conduct of that episode). The flagship's symbolism is more significant than its fire-power or even its size.

There is no doubting the potency of the image of cathedrals as 'flagships of the spirit'. One of our authors coined the phrase from his experience of looking down from the air upon the 600 parish churches of Norfolk. Each of them, he notes, points in the same direction, as if moored in some vast harbour, awaiting a fleet review. In the midst of them all stands Norwich Cathedral, like a great flagship, its spire standing as an ensign above the marshes of the River Wensum. It is not difficult to detect echoes of this image in other cathedrals throughout England: Lincoln bestrides the cliff like a great ocean liner; St Albans looks more like a supertanker at anchor; York Minster floats massively upon the calm waters of the surrounding plain; Durham holds its masts proudly above the River Wear; and Canterbury, with its noble Bell Harry Tower, is a symbolic flagship not only for the Church of England, but for the Anglican Communion world-wide. But it would be narrowing the view to restrict the symbolic power of cathedrals to Anglicanism. Often, with flags flying, they are symbols of the loyalty of people to their city, county or region, and are seen as significant by people of any Christian Church or none. The cathedrals in Salisbury, Truro and Coventry, and the two cathedrals in Liverpool (these last three from our modern age) speak powerfully to the cities and regions in which they are set. The urban parish-church cathedrals in Portsmouth, Sheffield, Manchester, Chelmsford and elsewhere have helped to articulate the fears and aspirations essential to the contemporary industrial and commercial landscape. Seen from the very best point of view, then, cathedrals can be described as 'flagships of the spirit'.

Sadly, however, cathedrals have not always been seen from the best point of view. In 1877, for example, Edward White Benson, then archbishop of Canterbury, wrote:

> Thirty years ago cathedral bodies were in the very depth of unpopularity. Nothing but some Heaven-born instinct in the English people then prevented their extinction . . . The most far-reaching, the most effectively and beautifully constituted, but lately most influential Christian institutions of the country had been enervated, paralysed, devitalized until the basest appointments to their honours could injure them no further.[1]

Benson's words capture perfectly the apparent ineffectiveness of cathedrals in mid-Victorian times, but his words capture also that 'Heaven-born instinct in the English people' which still seemed to view these places as potential flagships of the spirit. Fifty years later, Benson's successor at Canterbury, Cosmo Gordon Lang, had hardly a more sanguine view of cathedrals and their ministry:

> The cathedral, though once again the House of God, has still to win its place as the mother, the central church of the whole diocese to which the tribes of the Lord, the people from its towns and villages, go up with gladness. In many dioceses and in many parishes the cathedral is still a place remote and strange. Individuals may enter it sometimes, but it has little place of its own in the corporate life of the Church.[2]

Without a doubt the situation has changed since both these archbishops wrote. Indeed it was Benson, when he was chancellor of Lincoln Cathedral and then later when he was bishop of Truro and dean of his own cathedral, who did much to spearhead the vanguard of cathedral reform. He was particularly keen to put cathedrals on the map as diocesan churches. Within his schema, the canons of the cathedral would look after educational, social and pastoral work in the diocese. The establishment of Lincoln Theological College as a re-foundation of the Scholae Cancellarii (a reflection of medieval schools attached to Lincoln and other cathedrals) was all part of Benson's vision. In the first quarter of this century Frank Bennett added to Benson's work, when he became dean of Chester. Bennett's vision, however, was not identical to Benson's. At one point he wrote:

> By a real cathedral I mean a great central family house of God, through which, and through its many essential chapels, the diocese can express its manifold corporate life, under the shadow and in the inspiration of which it can do its rapidly increasing business, and in which or near which it can find refreshment for soul and body. At Chester we have just decided to move our diocesan offices into a house adjacent to our refectory and cloister, where we shall enjoy hereafter, and all under the same roof, a spaciousness and convenience that many a city might covet for its municipal buildings.[3]

There is, of course, some overlap with Benson's vision: both saw the cathedral as the diocesan church. But Bennett's vision was still broader, as his reference to municipal buildings implies. Cathedrals were for the region. They were great buildings which, like no other such magnificent enclosed spaces, could host gatherings for the widest cross-section of people within the community. Both Benson and Bennett were quite clear, in subtly different ways, that cathedrals ought to be and could be flagships of the spirit.

Sociological and cultural shifts in the past 50 years have radically changed the landscape once again. Perhaps the single most significant change has been the explosion of the tourist industry. In the past 20 years, for example, the number of people visiting Canterbury Cathedral has trebled to the present figure of about 2.25 million people per year. Canterbury may be an extreme case, with its proximity to the cross-Channel ferries and the Channel Tunnel, and as the focal point of the world-wide Anglican Communion. Yet much the same could be said about tourist numbers in the majority of medieval English cathedrals. Cathedrals have had no choice but to respond to this drastically changed situation. Hospitality, interpretation and welcome for visitors is now near the top of their agendas. Inner city, parish-church cathedrals have also broadened their focus of work, and in some cases have taken initiatives towards bold developments aimed at drawing in a wider public. Often cathedrals have joined in partnership with civic authorities, not only in the realm of tourism, but also in offering themselves as an effective centre for the life of the city, county and region. They have attempted to realise their potential as flagships of the spirit.

Both the history outlined above, and these contemporary challenges, have led the authors of this book to reflect on a variety of aspects of cathedral life. There has been much new thinking about the role, function and *raison d'être* of cathedrals at the turn of this millennium, in addition to a revision of the legislation governing their lives. The essays here are not intended as prescriptive nor necessarily as prophetic. Some essays have a stronger historical bias; some concentrate more specifically on contemporary analysis of the life and work of cathedrals. They are all written, however, with the conviction that cathedrals have an essential part to play in the mission of the Church and in the life of contemporary society. Although the writers contributing to this volume consulted each other before embarking on their essays, this is not a 'committee effort' – nor, indeed, has there been an attempt to impose any identical structure upon the various contributions which comprise the book. It is, however, our hope that this corporate reflection has given this collection some consistency in our understanding of the task in hand. The essays are not offered as a historical analysis of the development of cathedrals –

although history plays its necessary part in a number of the essays. We also recognise the variety of tasks and the multiplicity of challenges in the kaleidoscopic landscape which makes up cathedral life in England: there is no one blueprint. How, precisely, then, have we approached our task?

The first two essays should be seen rather differently from those which follow. From two very different standpoints, these two contributions attempt to set the context. Susan Hill, starting with intimate knowledge of one particular cathedral, approaches cathedrals from the perspective of a novelist. She appreciates the work of cathedrals but also points to dangers. Christopher Rowland combines his skills as a biblical theologian with a love of cathedrals issuing from his own experience; and yet, as he indicates, the image of the Temple has always been ambivalent in the Judaeo-Christian tradition. Thereafter the essays explore different aspects of the cathedral tradition. Nicolas Alldrit reflects on the communities that have given birth to cathedrals and the lessons that these community models may have for us today. David Stancliffe looks at the liturgical use of cathedrals and at what this may say of our ecclesiological models. Richard Shephard examines some of the myths and aspirations of the cathedral musical tradition, and Andrew Anderson takes an oblique view of the buildings themselves and of the architecture that has fashioned them. Keith Walker makes a strong plea for the Church (and cathedrals especially) once again to become effective patrons of the arts. He also wishes the Church to reclaim a more profound understanding of the place of art in its sacramental ecclesiology. Stephen Platten analyses the theological origins of cathedrals and of their role in contemporary society, while Christopher Lewis and gives a sociological and theological reflection on the effects of cathedral life on those who pass through these buildings. Angela Tilby's essay places the life and work of cathedrals within a phenomenological understanding of humankind's search for meaning and for the divine Spirit. The final essay is offered as a reflection upon the whole book and upon the implications of the thinking brought together here: what might all this imply about cathedrals in the coming century? The collection is offered not simply to cathedrals, but to the Church and to wider society in the belief that these buildings have an essential part to play in nurturing the religious life of the nation – they ought indeed to be flagships of the spirit.

ONE

AT THE STILL POINT OF THE TURNING WORLD

Cathedrals experienced

SUSAN HILL

It is very early one morning. The world beyond the precincts has just begun to stir. Nearby, in trees and gardens, the birds are madly singing, and because it is so quiet within, although these walls are made of stone a foot thick, you can just hear them. Later, it may be very hot. But never in here.

Arches. Dim corners. Cool shadows. Space. The nave. The chancel. The side aisles. The transept. The choir. The presbytery. Somewhere below, the chapterhouse. Rood screen. Clerestory. Cloisters. Strange words. You might need a dictionary to discover what they mean. Anything?

Sun lancing through high windows. Look up. It is like being Jonah inside the belly of the whale. The rib-cage surrounds you. You see the bones. The neck soars up out of sight, to a world elsewhere.

You sit then. Or kneel. The light falling through violet and emerald and rose and umber and turquoise makes a rainbow on the plain stone slabs. Dust dances. Golden motes.

There are footsteps. The swish of a garment. The scrape of a match. Small tongues of flame flicker above the great candles, catching the silver, the gold, the brass. And then the voice

1

begins, murmuring quietly, soothingly, the cadences like the coming and going of the sea. A second voice in reply.

'In the name of the Father and of the Son and of the Holy Ghost.'

'Amen.'

The first service of the day. The first prayer, breaking into the huge hollow silence of these spaces. Holy spaces.

The priest. The attendant. Plain, in plain robes. Bare headed.

In the long nave, perhaps two or three gathered together.

So, this is a cathedral. Now. Or then. Tomorrow. Today. A hundred years ago. A thousand, even.

This space, these people. These voices murmuring. It is vast. Almost empty. Yet if you had come in quite alone, if there had been no priest, no server, no other human being at all, it is certain, strangely, that you would not have felt an emptiness. A cathedral is never empty. Why is this? The imprint of a thousand years of prayers, voices, footsteps? Who else is here, for company?

But it does not need this mighty space, this extravagance of stone, this breathtaking piece of the builder's art, to contain two people saying prayers before two or three others.

This is something beyond the necessary, then.

Who are you, who have come quietly here at this early morning. Why? Why here? It is possible that here, you do not feel exposed, known, as you might in a small church. Here you may lose yourself among the pillars and be known to no one. No one?

Here, if you choose not to join in, no one may observe it, no one will remark. Instead you may simply stand on the sidelines. The brink. (Of what?) Ask questions. (Of whom?)

At such times, the cathedral may be a place of refuge. From

what? 'The weariness, the fever and the fret.' Of course. From the night's work, perhaps done in the midst of other people's pain, loneliness, distress, fear. Or merely in the midst of machinery, a din and a racket.

Or it may be to gather strength and steadfastness with which to face the coming day. Or inspiration. Or solutions.

A place of preparation, then.

'Go in peace.'

At the heart of this space at early morning, as the quiet words thread in and out, all around you in the air pierced by the early morning sun, is what is necessary. You may take it. Silence. Strength. Solutions. The sense of a presence.

But in the middle of this glory, towering to heaven, is a plainness, a sense of the ordinary and the usual. Familiar words spoken. They give reassurance. They do not change. And yet suddenly, caught, heard for the first time – or as if for the first time – they are words that may change one utterly.

❧

Or else it is evening. In the bleak mid-winter. The world beyond the cathedral streams with lights and crowds, roars with frustration, impatience, weariness, dissatisfaction. It is bitterly cold.

But not in here. Nowadays, the cathedral is quite warm – a relief to those who do come in. Though there are still only two or three. (It is all a question of time.)

Sunlight does not break in now. Above you, the infinitely dark spaces. Shadows alongside. And the two figures, the two lit candles, the same murmur of words.

'Lord, now lettest thou thy servant depart in peace according to thy word.'

This morning, the building was expectant. Now, it gathers

in the discarded threads of the day, and binds them together –
the going in and out, the bustle and words and music, the
workaday things. The pilgrims passing through. The mourners,
perhaps. The important people, on business.

All have gone.

Who is here now? Why? For the beauty of the words,
certainly. Truths, solemnly spoken. The release of whatever
tensions. For escape. In gratitude. The old may come because
they are drawn to the comfort of one old man's valediction.
The sense of rounding-off, of a day, of a life.

Whatever happens in this immensity now is private. Un-
shared but still gathered in. Burdens may be dropped from
your back and left here. They will be gathered in too. You will
see them no more.

You do not arrive here by chance or leave here unaffected.

In this place, built by the vision and cunning and sweat of
men, are only these few. But they are equally valid, of equal
significance.

And their being here is of eternal significance, and the building's daily justification. They may stand for all others.

'Lighten our darkness, we beseech thee O Lord; and by thy
great mercy defend us from all perils and dangers of this
night.'

For someone coming by chance into the cathedral, in the quietness, early or late, these may be times of importance. Of
reflection, stillness, crisis, change.

But surely there are many places that will serve the purpose?
To which people may come freely, to be alone among others. To
pray, to reflect, to plead, gather strength, rest, summon up
courage; to listen to solemn words.

What are these other places? To which the pilgrim or the
traveller, the seeker, the refugee, the petitioner or the thanks-

giver, may quietly come, anonymously, perhaps, without fear of comment or remark, question or disturbance?

Where are these places?

❧

But the cathedral is not always quiet, still, dim and full of space and shadows. There are the great occasions. Then, it is vibrant with light and music, every seat is taken, there are fanfares of trumpets, the organ is triumphant, the people are in procession, the notes seek out the furthest, highest corners, and pierce them brilliantly. On such days there is no hiding place. Instead, there is splendour, and men go by their proudest names wearing silk and fine linen, mitres and stoles of gold and silver, carrying staffs. The priests are resplendent. Men and boys wear skirts and lace. No one in the sought-after seats wishes to be anonymous. It is a day for kings and prelates and a well-rehearsed, immaculate performance.

The cathedral is never short of great occasions and people wanting to come as an audience, as spectators. 'Congregation' is too ordinary, too humble, a word. They might be called worshippers – though of what is uncertain.

The man in the glittering mitre and golden cope, carrying the jewelled staff, wearing the rings. Is he a king, come to his palace? Is this seat his throne?

Wasn't there talk of another king?

Who is the naked, broken man with nails driven into his feet and hands, hanging there in the shadows on a cross. What has he to do with all of this? Has he any place at such a show?

The performance is superb. Impressive. Breathtaking. Everything is of the finest. Everyone excels. It is a solemn celebration.

Is it a performance? No one applauds, and admission today

5

is by ticket and coveted invitation: no one has paid entrance money. A grand party, then? But why hold it here?

It is an occasion for rejoicing. For offering the finest, the richest, the rarest, the most splendid. The best that can be offered.

Offered? To whom?

Many another place would hold the crowd, provide the same facilities. Yet strangely it is thought that no other place would do.

No other could bring to this mighty, processional occasion the essence of all other such occasions from the past, their spirit, their meaning and purpose, pressed, crystallised, distilled, present somehow in the very air, the stones, the atmosphere. This is no mere spectacle, however fine.

Because it has taken place here, strangely, the word 'service' can still apply. And in the midst of the pomp and ceremonial are the familiar, plain words, spoken and sung, said or heard, and the words can break free and strike home, here, or there, through the best clothes, the silks, the formal uniforms and robes, the elaborate hats. So that even as they look on and admire and are impressed, some may be touched and taken unawares – taken aback, perhaps by the quick sight of the broken man in the half-shadow, as well as raised up by the glory of the music, the splendour, the solemnity. The building itself, which stands as it has stood for all these years at the heart of the city, and into which they may never have been.

People have come proudly, expecting to be impressed. But sitting here they are caught up unexpectedly in some other wonder. And there are pauses, in which some may ask questions, about those who built this cathedral, and those who keep it alive. And why.

But of course, for the most part, days are ordinary days. If the word ordinary can ever apply to this cathedral whose beauty catches the breath.

It is often 11 o'clock on a mid-week morning, mid-year, mid-season, not Christmas, Easter, or any particular feast or festival. What is the purpose of the cathedral now? Is anyone here? When any other church or chapel will be empty, silent (dead?), the cathedral will be humming with ordinary, workaday life. Visitors gazing, guides describing, organ tuners playing upon a single note relentless as toothache, flower arrangers dropping a metal vase with a ring that echoes round and round up into the roof spaces, men in hard hats importantly discussing scaffold. Through this door, the refectory – coffee and cake for shoppers. (Refreshment for pilgrims then.) Through that door, the shop. Trinkets, souvenirs. (Bibles, prayer books. God and Mammon then. Money lenders and changers in the Temple?)

No one leaves this building unmoved, by the sheer size and strength and space and glory of it. Stand here and you stand in the middle of a mighty work of art, a great feat of engineering – call it what you wish, it will envelop you. And what strikes you is that it is not quite the same as a palace, a museum, a gallery, a hall, a mausoleum.

There is something else.

Call it a sense of presence. Of holiness. Awe and reverence are the words which apply. But they are tempered. You may walk in quietly and freely here. You will not be challenged, except by the unseen, the unexpected. You have as much right to be here as anyone. You will not be rejected for failing to have the right pass, passport, password, coin, face, name, uniform. Or the right reason.

Refuge and sanctuary are also words that apply.

The cathedral is more than the sum of its parts.

Look at it another way.

Fifty years ago, there were so many sparrows bathing in bowls of dust or puddles in the road, you could never count. So many swallows and martins gathering on wires and ledges you could scarcely put a pin between them. So many thousands of larks, rinsing the air, spiralling upwards through the spring. So many warblers, tits, grebes, martins, wagtails, owls, hawks, eagles, finches, thrushes, waders, peewits following the plough. So many billions of wrens. So many. Were not two sparrows sold for a farthing?

So many fewer now. Now, we can count the few swallows spaced out along the wires, mark the absence of sparrows. The silent skies. We have woken up to the terrible truth, that we may face a future without birds.

It is unimaginable. We took them for granted. We took them.

Grandmother said you never know the value of what you have until it's gone.

Durham. Westminster. Wells. Norwich. Exeter. Salisbury. Canterbury. St Paul's. Picture them. Click. Picture them gone. The idea of their absence is an absence in the heart; not an airy emptiness, a leaden one. It is a deadness. To think of the world without these cathedrals, without all cathedrals, is like a bereavement. It is painful. The loss of the buildings themselves, the grandeur, the beauty, is unimaginable – the mind veers away from it. But think of the world without the great palaces. Surely that is just the same?

We know, deeply, instinctively, that it is not. Destroy all the churches then? Is that not the same?

We know that it is more. And that it is not merely a question of size. Nor of the fear of thunderbolts.

I have come at the idea of a cathedral sideways, as it were, and tentatively, asking questions. Dogmatism does not seem a very useful approach, or one that appeals much to our way of thinking. It is by questioning, trying to find different perspectives from which to look at things – coming at them sideways – that we often work our way towards new meanings and solutions.

We are born to ask questions. That is how we learn, change, develop, grow, mature, make sense of our journey and its purpose. When we are children, we ask questions as naturally as we breathe, but we get out of the way of it as we become adult. Of course, the tendency to ask questions – and particularly the most challenging question, 'Why?' – may merely be a sign of cussedness and an adolescent refusal to accept any received ideas or the *status quo*, just because that is what they are. Yet if we are open-minded, asking 'Why?' may be the means by which, perhaps to our own surprise, we come to understand that the very *status quo*, received ideas, beliefs, standards, still have validity – are 'relevant' to us. Or, of course, they may not. At any rate, the question must be asked. It is just that we may not pre-empt the answer, that is all.

❧

I write from the position of a questioning outsider who feels perfectly at home inside the cathedral. I know a number from a visitor's viewpoint: their settings and situation, architecture, the works of art they contain, their atmosphere and a little of their history. They are moving beyond words, mighty tributes to the cunning of man, his skills, vision, faith, far-sightedness, and unselfishness of purpose. Like most people I cannot now picture the world in their absence, or easily sum up what their loss would mean. Think of the film when some huge, unsafe structure, some tower block or chimney, is blown up: the blast, the split second's freeze-frame, the slowly toppling pile; the cloud of dust. The rubble. The vacant space. Then think of that as being, one after the other, our cathedrals. See it. Durham. York. Norwich. Canterbury ...

Once, the unthinkable happened, to Coventry Cathedral in 1940.

On the same night that it was destroyed by enemy bombers, the decision was taken, amidst the still burning ruins, to resurrect it, as the new Coventry Cathedral. It is the only cathedral with which I have been associated other than as a sightseeing visitor. I worked there and was a member of the worshipping congregation for a time, shortly after its consecration in 1962. Then, the new Coventry Cathedral was self-consciously, proudly modern, of its day, up-to-date. Relevant. It looked back only to find its reason for looking forward and reaffirming itself.

The words associated with it were reconciliation, unity, peace – and those key words still apply. They are timeless words.

Otherwise, look at Coventry Cathedral and you look at a building that went out of date as soon as it was built. It is supremely of the 1950s. There is nothing at all 'of today' about it now. It has dated as the clothes and the furniture of its period have dated. That was inevitable. Much of its early pioneering work, many of its bold, brave attempts to break out of the mould of traditional Church and Christian thinking and action, seem dated too, just because they were so self-consciously 'of their day', 'modern', relevant. 'Contemporary.'

In a sense, that does not matter. It does not invalidate the cathedral's existence, nor much of the work – the prayer, the purpose – nor detract from the importance of the attempts it was making to ... well, to what? Probably it was to make people ask questions about the *status quo*, refuse to accept things on trust, just because they had always been said, done, thought, believed, that way.

Coventry may have a particular importance as a pointer to

the situation of our cathedrals now. And as something of a warning.

But if so, it is certainly not because questions were asked.

Cathedrals feel insecure. Once again, we feel that the old certainties cannot be relied upon, the ground has shifted beneath our feet, questions are being asked. What is the purpose of a cathedral today? What is its point, relevance, justification? Is anything that goes on in it of use and value to people about to enter the next century? Cathedrals fret about such questions, because they make them feel insecure. If you doubt yourself, if you feel your house is built upon a certain amount of sand, you are anxious. And so they fret once again about being modern, up-to-date, of their time. They mind desperately what people think. They would not have done so once. They were supremely confident of their own validity, point and purpose when they were built.

Now, they try to reassure themselves that they still have a purpose in a hundred ways, perhaps by making themselves more comfortable, or by bolting on new visitor centres, by being seen as politically correct, joining anxiously in the debates about relevance and justification, worrying about appearances. Money. Criticism.

Perhaps they should stop worrying, and see themselves rather as above their own time, out of time, timeless, committed simply to the eternal, unchanging spiritual values, eternal human needs, supremely, sublimely confident again in their own *raison d'être*.

Perhaps they waste too much energy running as fast as they can to keep up.

Most cathedrals are 'old', but the life that takes place within them is endlessly renewed, endlessly of the eternal present. And the words which can apply to them are timeless words, not words merely of today. Silence. Prayer. Stillness. Refuge.

Holy. Sacred. Strength. Devotion. Sanctuary. Quietness. Assurance. Those are some of the words. Others are to be heard spoken in their daily prayer. What cathedrals have to offer the modern world are those things for which they were built, which they have always had to offer. Those are the point of their existence.

People hunger and thirst after many things, but most especially after respite and refuge; from noise, change, disturbance, transience, overcrowding, insecurity, Mammon, stress, pollution, dirt, fickleness, violence, anguish, competition, disillusionment, struggle, failure, and they long for relief from those things even more strongly because they sense that there is the possibility of finding it.

But they do not find what they need – all comfort, reassurance, strength, peace – within the confines of organised religion and dogma and formal ways of worship.

Yet if increasingly they reject these, they do not reject the idea of the life of the spirit, they continue to search for that respite, that refuge, that solace. How otherwise to explain the rampant New Ageism? And the attraction of retreats into silent, remote places, of religions of passivity such as Buddhism – even the surging popularity of Gregorian chant? I do not think we should dismiss hunger for such things as superficial and sentimental.

Is it time for cathedrals to stop and ask questions about their anxious attempts to be relevant and up-to-date? Perhaps the questions may lead to a turning away from the present, back towards the past, to rediscover the values upon which their foundations are set, and which are timeless, out of time, above time.

There is something extraordinarily powerful about the simplicity of the monastic ideal and way, the appeal of silence, quietness, solitude, simplicity, of moderation, plainness, sense of community, commitment to giving refuge and shelter. It is in part an aesthetic appeal, partly the attraction of contrast and of a spiritual stripping-away. The monastic way is unchanging and therefore always relevant, utterly self-confident, rooted in eternal spiritual values.

What other places have the power and the space and the confidence to offer a contrast to the weariness, the fever and the fret – quiet, magnificent, simple spaces to which all may come freely for refreshment, strength, solace, sanctuary; and the answers to questions. The life of the monastery continues on behalf of the world, whether that world chooses to come to it or to ignore it. It is quite sure of itself and of its own point and purpose.

Where else in the heart of a city is such a place, where the sense of all past, all present, is distilled into the eternal moment 'at the still point of the turning world'?

The cathedral is its own justification, offering the words of the Bible, the services of the prayer book and prayer on behalf of the city in which it stands, and providing the prayer-filled silence and emptiness of its great spaces unchangingly.

(Is it enough to cordon off some dim corner in which those at private prayer may feel as exposed to gaze as creatures in a zoo?)

In Roman Catholic countries, the atmosphere of what might be called 'ordinary holiness' in the great cathedrals is maintained, even in the presence of a thousand visitors. The sense of the presence of God, the reverence of those in prayer, communicate themselves, and are moving and impressive. So are the great branches of candles stuck about with fluttering notes on which so many private petitions are written, and the sight of those who so piously light fresh ones. If we are seekers not believers, such faith makes us stop, think, ask questions, to which tentative answers may sometimes be found in the cool darkness – which is itself such a respite from the bright, hot world outside. There is an instinctive code about how we behave in such places which does not seem strange, does not seem repressive. Children are welcome, babies cry and toddlers totter between the stone pillars. But women cover their heads, and a certain modesty of dress is expected. We once took such an atmosphere, such ways, for granted. We could restore it. The buildings will help us. It may not be difficult. Perhaps it is only a question of taking the decision.

Perhaps it is all a question of maintaining tensions. Of balance.

How to maintain the tension between the holy, the sense of otherness, the silence, the awareness of the presence of God, the sacred space, the eternal present – and the temporary now, which also concerns us; between an openness to the everyday affairs and troubles of humankind, and our eternal needs; between being a part and being apart? There is a tension in the one who comes to the cathedral. Can the visitor be in awe of the building, of the sense of the presence of God, the atmosphere of prayerfulness, and yet also feel at home there, at ease, welcome and not intimidated? Surely, for holy buildings – the synagogue, the mosque, the abbey, the temple – have a long history and an instinctive way of making the stranger feel welcome.

The tension between all these needs can be recognised, and then maintained. It was not a problem once. Then, cathedrals were confident, knowing that they were their own justification. They did not feel any need to apologise. They were of their time and out of time.

Perhaps it is the ceremonies, the grand occasions, for which the outsider can see no reason, the ostentatious display of ecclesiastical treasures, the men in frocks of gold and lace. They are rejected by some as merely pointless, by others as risible; but, more seriously, by many as being offensive. The pomp and ceremony are both off-putting and puzzling; those who do not belong, and many who do, feel as alienated from the pomp and pomposity, in the odd, theatrical garments, as they do from the displays and trappings of royalty. But the best of our offerings, the best music, the most magnificent words, do not alienate and are not seen as mere extravagance: such things are their own justification and are recognised as offerings of excellence – as are the buildings themselves.

People do not come to the cathedral because it is the same as other places, but because it is not. The sacred spaces and the holy silences are rare and precious, to be broken into and disturbed rarely and only with good reason. There is sometimes a purpose in the splendid ceremony, just as there is a point to the celebration of our rites of passage. Perhaps it is the word 'sometimes' that best applies.

There is another tension, then, between providing a refuge and a sanctuary, a respite, a contrast, not restricting access or turning away or charging even the multitudes of the most tiresome sightseers – and between frowning upon anything that does wantonly break into the silence and that sense of otherness, holiness, set-apartness, prayerfulness. Think of the cost of the cathedral – not financial, but human – the cost in the years of peoples' lives and often, those lives themselves, of the wear on their bodies, their backs, arms, hands. Vision and labour and sacrifice and generosity indeed. We owe it to them to put the highest value on the legacy we have received, to take seriously the questions we must ask about it; we hold the cathedrals in trust on their behalf, for now and for the future.

❧

We do not need any more cathedrals. That seems clear. Who could possibly justify another Coventry today? – for all that Coventry was eminently justifiable, a triumph of hope at the darkest hour, of defiance, and confidence in the future; a triumph of belief and reaffirmation, in the Church and in the purpose of a cathedral, in the idea of reconciliation and of community, of belief in contemporary art and church patronage; perhaps above all a triumph of the symbolic.

But we have no room for more. Our world is too full of buildings. The expense could not be justified. There is not the need.

And can the monstrous expense of maintaining our existing cathedrals be justified? What need is there for those?

We have no right wantonly to destroy great works; we have a duty to conserve them, whether they are artefacts or buildings. The cathedrals are part of our inheritance. That much is obvious, it is the only civilised reply. But it is one that applies equally to palaces, castles, museums. In a hostile world, the cathedrals have to look for a greater justification even than these for their existence. For the hostility does not come only from without. One argument against them comes from within, at their very own heart, for it is based persuasively on Christian teaching. It brings to the attack a wealth of powerful references, about not laying up stores of treasure on earth and the difficulty camels might have in passing through the eyes of needles; it refers to golden idols, and instructions about selling all and giving to the poor and considering the lilies of the field ... And indeed, it is true that, taken alone, the ostentatious display of glittering treasures and garments, jewels and plate, when the cathedral is in full, processional mode may be offensive, seen in the context of the beggars at the gate and beyond the precincts.

But was there not a woman who broke open a jar of precious ointment to pour extravagantly over a man's head? It seems that neither side has a monopoly on supportive quotations. There are those who say most stridently that our cathedrals cannot be justified by any reference to the New Testament.

But there is more to God than the New Testament. The Holy Spirit bloweth where it listeth. Even through the silent spaces of the cathedral. It will not be confined within the pages of a book. Even that book. Even this.

TWO

FRIENDS OF ALBION?

The danger of cathedrals

CHRISTOPHER ROWLAND

William Blake, in *Jerusalem*, called the English cathedral cities 'the friends of Albion' (Albion being the embodiment of Britain in Blake's idiosyncratic myth).[1] What kind of friends are being talked of here? Are they merely companions who go along with every whim and desire of their friend, or are they those who have the true interests of their friend at heart and are prepared to talk about those things that make for their friend's peace and well-being? Blake's poem suggests that they behave as the former, but should be acting in the latter capacity. Too many of them are infected with the same disease which eventually kills Albion, despite the prophetic call to recognise their mission. The disease is a religion of sacrifice, of rules, which lacks mutual forgiveness and the promotion of human kinship. Like the rest of the inhabitants of Albion, the friends either collude with, or promote, life committed to the senses and without the transforming power of imagination, and so they betray true art which is the gateway to the eternal and to a set of values.

Blake had the highest regard for the Gothic artists who built the medieval cathedrals, seeing them as persons fired by imagination. But, despite exceptional prophetic spirits who emerged from some of the cathedrals, he saw that the Christian religion was severely compromised by the cathedrals' cultural ethos, and opposed to the way of Jesus. The cathedrals point to a God of 'mercy, pity, peace and love', and yet often seem entangled in the values of a world opposed to God, as Jerusalem and Babylon mingle together. They are touched by God's Spirit and can offer a glimpse of another dimension to existence, while at the same time they are tainted with barbarism and based on 'the anonymous toil of their contemporaries', as Walter Benjamin put it.[2]

Blake's ambivalence towards cathedrals is shared by many, both inside and outside the Christian Churches. We can go into these wonderful buildings and may catch in them a glimpse of eternity – but in their structures, in their particular relationship with society at large, and in their seeming cultivation of privilege in worship and life, they seem to be opposed to the values of the Lamb of God. That ambivalence is reflected in various parts of the biblical tradition which pose serious theological questions about church buildings, including cathedrals, in the life of the people of God. To paraphrase a recent Church of England report: the criticism of worldly splendour, which lay at the heart of the Cistercian ideal, leads one to ask whether the glory of the medieval cathedrals is really the most authentic representation of the religion of Galilean fishermen or Francis of Assisi.[3]

There is therefore a serious theological issue concerning the nature and operation of cathedrals which is often ignored or by-passed, perhaps because it seems to have been settled long ago. Churches which hear the Scriptures and seek to respond to them will, however, sooner or later find a discrepancy between contemporary practice and key aspects of the scriptural vision. Of course, questions are raised about all sacred places, and the attitudes of Christians to them – not just cathedrals. Cathedrals, because of their place in a nation's culture and affections, offer an acute example of the wider theological problem. Even if I were competent to do so, I can hope to do no more than scratch the surface of a subject which deserves the sort of treatment in our day given to it by Bede, our great ancestor in the faith.[4] My particular interest is biblical studies, and it is to the scriptural witness that I turn to suggest that we cannot easily side-step the theological challenge to our attitudes to buildings, nor ignore the questions it poses to our practice.

In the Torah, provision for liturgy centres on the tabernacle, though the ancestors had worshipped regularly at a variety of holy places. As with human monarchy, which has an important though ambiguous position in the history of the people of God (1 Sam. 8; 2 Sam. 7:14), the role of the Temple and (more often) of other places of religious worship is viewed with a mixture of approbation, unease and downright condemnation. Despite the divine sanction for the building of the Temple in Jerusalem and its conformity to the divine plan (1 Chron. 28:12, 19), the description of the building of the Temple suggests that, from its very inception, its structures were infused by the spirit of Canaan. 1 Kings 11 records Solomon's departure from the worship of God, continued in the deeds of his descendants which, in the books of Kings, becomes a litany of catastrophic decline from the single-minded devotion to the God of Israel's ancestors. The story of the books of Kings would have been familiar to Blake: Temple worship involved compromise with local cults, with the world of the senses and with the values of the settled society of the Canaanite cities. God who is beyond human comprehension, recognised as such in Solomon's prayer in 1 Kings 8:27, came to be too closely identified with a place, a temple made with hands (1 Kings 8; Isa. 66:1f, quoted in Acts 7:49f), a dynasty, a city – and perhaps inevitably with oppression and injustice. God's approval of the building did not extend to the form, content and actions in it, as the conditions laid out in the response to Solomon's prayer make clear (1 Kings 9:3). The Temple, decorated and influenced as it was by the culture of Canaan, rapidly became a shrine to Baal and not to Yahweh.

As the years went by, the extent of this departure from God's purposes was recognised from time to time, particularly in the reigns of Hezekiah and Josiah. There appears to have been a lack of awareness, among elites and people alike, of the extent of the discrepancy between the practice of the Temple and the demands of God. There were those who kept the Sinaitic vision alive: a vision of a people formed in the desert, who had shed the false consciousness of Egypt and its fleshpots, but who had not yet been corrupted by Canaanite life. Theirs was a vision of a God who required concern for the orphan, the widow and the stranger, and whose presence was particularly connected with the portable tabernacle rather than the permanent and glorious edifice of the Temple. The Exodus vision had almost disappeared in the Jerusalem of the monarchic period. It makes only a rare appearance in the psalmody of Solomon's Temple and in the oracles of Jerusalem's prophets. Even the celebration of the Passover had fallen into desuetude (2 Kings 23:22). In place of the story of the Exodus and the giving of the Law, the myths of the Davidic dynasty (together with the invincibility of Zion and its Temple) so dominated the culture that the austere story of the formation of a people with a religion of tabernacle and social justice was almost forgotten. Prophets like Isaiah called a people to seek justice, rescue the oppressed, defend the orphan, plead for the widow, rather than 'the multitude of your sacrifices' (Isa. 1:11, 17). The prophetic critique reaches its climax in Ezekiel and Jeremiah, when Solomon's Temple is regarded as a place of idolatry, nowhere more stingingly rebuked than in Jeremiah's Temple sermon (Ezek. 8:5ff; Jer. 7:4, 8f).

We can only guess what a shock it must have been to the Temple culture which echoed the conviction, 'God is in the midst of the city; it shall never be moved' (Ps. 46:5), when the Temple was destroyed after the invasion of Nebuchadnezzar. After the return from exile there seems to have been a struggle between those like Haggai and Zechariah, who wanted to see the Temple rebuilt as a symbol of Israel's life, and those who held out against such a move with a grander vision, more universal in scope. Haggai prophesies that the impoverishment of Israel is the result of the neglect of 'old-fashioned' Temple religion. If only the Temple were rebuilt (and scarce resources thereby diverted to the restoration of cultic activity), then all would be well in the land (Hag. 1:4ff). It is likely that the oracles which make up the final chapters of Isaiah bear witness to the growing disillusionment of a prophetic group who find themselves outmanoeuvred by the protagonists of Temple reconstruction, and thus marginalised in Israel's life. As Jews sought to survive in the hostile world of ancient Near Eastern power politics, figures like Ezra and Nehemiah consolidated the life of Jerusalem centred around priesthood, Temple and Law. But, as even Nehemiah 5 indicates, there can be no escape from the priority given to social justice, with the ruling elite, in the person of Nehemiah, taking the lead. The Temple continued to play a central role in the lives of Jews, both inside and outside Judaea, in the years preceding the Christian era. The regular flow of income to the Temple from all parts of the Roman empire led to the enrichment of this institution and those who ran it. It was the focus of religion, and was a powerful economic factor in Judaean life as well as an influential ideological symbol. But the Temple's pre-eminent place should not lead us to forget the evidence of the questioning of the Temple which continued in the intertestamental literature.

The priests who held power in Jerusalem preserved the Temple as a holy space at the heart of Jewish life in the holy city, in order to maintain the pattern of worship that they believed God had prescribed for that place. All that might defile the holy place was excluded from the Temple. In Jesus' day the maintenance of the cult necessitated some kind of coexistence with the Roman authorities (cf. John 11:48). This priority for the preservation of the holy place was highest on the agenda. Small wonder that, with the destruction of this holy place, the *raison d'être* of priestly religion should perish with the sacrifices they were pledged to preserve. The maintenance of a holy space was not, however, confined to the Temple. During the period of the Second Temple, this search for a holy space was carried out in a variety of ways. The members of the Qumran sect lived in the desert, and in their common life created a holy environment where the holy angels assembled and shared their life. The Pharisees' view of holiness was rooted in practical living in the midst of the variety of human communities, both near to and far from the Temple. The detailed regulations of the Mishna, the earliest code of Jewish practice outside the Bible, bear witness to the seriousness of the endeavour of their rabbinic successors to ensure the preservation of a holy space in all aspects of existence. It was that vision which enabled Judaism to survive the destruction of its holy place in 70 CE and for Pharisaism to become the driving force of what was to emerge in the second century as rabbinic Judaism.

Pharisees, like other Jews and Christians, may have been devastated by the destruction of the Temple in 70, but the emerging practice of religion based on the synagogue (which could meet anywhere and was not necessarily attached to particular places which were deemed to be holy) was a factor in enabling them to survive the events of 70. Buildings did not, in the last resort, matter in the life of the people of God; what mattered was obedience to the divine Law in all circumstances. Judaism has survived without a Temple for the last 2000 years. Judaism has maintained a religion which does not depend on Temple or even holy places, so paralleling the words of the third-century Christian writer, Minucius Felix: 'We have no temples; we have no altars'.[5] Judaism contrasts with what the Christian religion has become.

Initially, the early Christians shared the ambivalent relationship to the Temple evident in some Jewish circles during the Second Temple period (e.g. Acts 6:13; cf. Mark 14:58; John 4:23). On the one hand, we find them using its imagery to describe their common life, hinting that this life replaces the holy life of the Temple in Jerusalem. On the other hand, some of the earliest Christians continued to worship in the Temple. The gospels leave us with a picture of Jesus who, in the last days of his life, prophesied the demise of the Temple. According to the gospel of Mark, Jesus' death comes at the end of a narrative in which, from Chapter 11 onwards, the Temple is a dominant theme. Jesus enters the Temple. In Mark the story of the cursing of the fig tree, which sandwiches the 'cleansing', is a comment on the bankruptcy of the institution. Its fate will be that of the cursed tree. Jesus condemns scribes for devouring widows' houses and, before leaving the Temple for the last time, gets his companions to note the way in which the widow, out of her poverty, puts in everything she has to live on, while the rest contributed out of their abundance (Mark 12:41ff). The incident is described without comment. But, in the light of Mark 12:40, where the scribes are condemned for devouring widows' houses, the fact that an institution allows an impoverished widow to give all that she has, sits uneasily with the demand in the Torah to care for the widow (Jer. 7:6; Deut. 24:17).

The death of Jesus is the moment when the heart of the old economic, political and religious institution is destroyed, truly 'the end of the world' for those who set great store by it. At his baptism a heavenly voice had proclaimed Jesus as God's son and the heavens were rent apart. So also is the veil of the Temple rent at Jesus' death (Mark 1:10; 15:38). Heaven and earth are linked at the rending of the heavens. But at the moment of Jesus' death, the tearing of the veil suggests something more destructive – the end of the Temple (cf. 1 Sam. 15:27). The veil, which symbolises the mystique of the Temple's power, is torn asunder signifying its demise. The Temple is replaced by a way of life based on service and an alternative 'holy space' focused on commemoration of Christ: 'in place of the Temple liturgy Jesus offers his body – that is, his messianic practice in life and death'.[6] The destruction means an end to an institution and an ideology which had dominated life, politically, religiously and economically. So the stones of the Temple, however beautiful, deserve no special attention except as monuments to an obsolescent form of religious life (Mark 13:2). In the days of Israel's exile the departure of the divine glory from the Temple was a sign of imminent destruction (Ezek. 1; 10). But, in contrast to Ezekiel's prophecy, there is no promise in the New Testament that any building would ever again be set apart as a particular place of the divine presence and worship – except 'the temple of Jesus' body' (John 2:21). The juxtaposition of death and rending at the climax of Mark's Gospel means that the moment of defeat of a prophet of the Temple's doom precipitates the institution's collapse. It is left to a representative of the Roman military to recognise in this moment the reign of another sort of king than Caesar (Mark 15:37; cf. Phil. 2:10f; John 18:36).

According to Acts, the first Christians continued to worship in the Temple, but in their articulation of the worship of God, the Temple had become a metaphor for the holiness and sense of divine presence in the lives of men, women and children. The importance of the physical Temple diminished, particularly in those texts which now form the canon of our New Testament: 'The hour is coming when you will worship the Father neither on this mountain nor in Jerusalem ... The true worshippers will worship the Father in spirit and truth, for the Father seeks such as these to worship him' (John 4:21, 23 NRSV). Among the early Christians are radical voices like Stephen's, whose implicit criticism of the Temple provokes a hostile reaction leading to his death. In the speech attributed to him in Acts, he dwells on the rebelliousness of the majority of his ancestors, and in his review of Israel's history he points to Solomon, who built a house for God which, if the quotation from Isaiah 66:1 is anything to go by, marked a departure from the divine intention; as the prophet says: 'Heaven is my throne, and the earth is my footstool. What kind of house will you build for me, says the Lord, or what is the place of my rest? Did not my hand make all these things?' (Acts 7:48 NRSV). Bede, in his 'De Templo', regards Stephen as a spiritual pioneer who explains to his hearers that 'the Lord does not place a high value on dressed stone, but rather desires the splendour of heavenly souls'.

Throughout the New Testament, sacred buildings, however glorious, seem to have been of little concern to its writers. Their prime concerns were the reign of God, the witness to the ways of God's justice, and the hope of heaven on earth, all anticipated in the common life of small groups of men, women and children. Christians began to explore a variant way of being God's people: their priority was the temple of the Holy Spirit, men and women of flesh and blood. Emmanuel, God with us, is met in the persons of the hungry, thirsty, naked and imprisoned, for the weak and marginal are the ones with whom Jesus identified (Matt. 1:23; 25:31ff). In the Pauline epistles we have glimpses of communities struggling to maintain a style of life at odds with contemporary culture. The locus of Christ's presence in the world is to be found in a variety of different places which share the holiness of God (1 Cor. 1:2ff; Rom. 12:1ff), and therefore where people seek to work as a community under God, distinguished by its quality of life and practical service (Rom. 15:25; 2 Cor. 8:4; Philem. 13). The community witnesses before the world at large, and maintains a 'divine presence' in the face of disregard for the justice of God (Rev. 10–11). Heaven and earth meet no longer in tabernacle or Temple, but outside the camp, a place of shame and reproach where the blasphemers and sabbath-breakers are stoned.[6] Those who share the way of Jesus can expect to go with him outside the camp, in the secular world.[7] God's love and solidarity is demonstrated in human beings in ways which the elaborate performance of cultic ritual never can be. The gate of heaven opens up to a solitary visionary on a Greek island (Rev. 1:9; 4:1), just as in the dark days of a people's exile in Babylon, when a prophet saw the divine glory move from above the cherubim in Solomon's Temple and encountered it in his place of exile by the waters of Babylon (Ezek. 1; 10). The unseen glory of cherubim and seraphim behind the veil in the Temple had burst beyond the veil. Despite the pessimism of the people who despaired of so doing, it was now possible to sing the Lord's song in a strange land. The Temple was superfluous as a witness to the divine presence. In the New Testament the human community is where God may now be found, acknowledged and served, and where the alternative vision of reality is maintained and celebrated. The hope in, and commitment to, the crucified Messiah, which are folly to humanity (1 Cor. 3:19), are incarnated in people where God's Spirit can dwell. But those communities of faithful people need to recognise that the divine often comes as a disturbing, apparently alien, presence, from outside the warmth of the gathered community. The risen Christ stands outside the door of a complacent Church and knocks, seeking entrance.

The sentiments of early Christian writers make disturbing reading, as Karl Barth appreciated in lectures of 1920:

> The church of the Bible is, significantly, the Tabernacle, the portable tent. The moment it becomes a Temple, it becomes essentially only an object of attack. One gathers that for the apostles the whole of the Old Testament is summarised in Stephen's apology. Undeniably the centre of interest of both Testaments is not in the building of the church but in its destruction, which is always threat-

ening and even beginning. In the heavenly Jerusalem of Revelation nothing is more finally significant than the church's complete absence: 'And I saw no Temple therein'.[8]

When Christianity became the religion of the Roman empire, things began to change. While some of the seeds of these developments antedate the Constantinian settlement, a significant shift took place after Constantine, whose reign offered fertile soil in which those seeds could grow. From about 260, but especially after 313, church buildings began to gain in size and become public structures. This reflected the growth in the size of congregations, and (after 313) of imperial favour. In the fourth century the Church grew, according to one estimate, from 10 per cent of the populace to about 50 per cent. Big buildings became necessary. Christians chose the basilica (associated with the emperor and with law courts) rather than the temple (associated with paganism) as the design template. So ecclesiastical buildings, which had hitherto been domestic (although getting larger), became public and were beautifully decorated to reflect imperial iconography. Space was divided into areas for clergy and laity. Because of the large congregations, the worship became large-scale rather than relational and communitarian.[9] As the number of worshippers grew and the places of worship likewise, ceremonial flourished and the importance of human relationship in divine service withered.[10]

So there begins to emerge a pattern of Christian activity which sits uneasily with the biblical vision of the common life. Passages in the Old Testament anticipate Blake's prophetic critique of the Anglicanism of his day, whose buildings, ethos and way of life had succumbed to a contemporary religion of Canaan, a culture of abstract reasoning and moral virtue. In the New Testament the identification of Christ with the Temple, and with the divine presence in unexpected places and persons, and the priority given to human relationships in ministry, leads us to widen our quest for the gates of heaven.

Supporters of cathedrals may well suggest that the money which goes to their appeals and which pays for the upkeep and pattern of worship would not go to the poor and needy. Nevertheless one has to ask what is the theological rationale for the huge expense involved in cathedral building and preservation. For example, a new cathedral is being built in Managua, Nicaragua, after the colonial building was destroyed in the 1972 earthquake. Why is this happening when hundreds of thousands are homeless, and half the population is without regular employment? One answer is to allude to the anointing at Bethany, or to say that it is the Judases of the world who complain about the expense while saying that the money should be given to the poor.[11] Such building projects can be replicated in other poor countries throughout the world – although by way of contrast, in the archdiocese of São Paulo which is a pioneer of the Roman Catholic Church's 'preferential option for the poor', the bishop's palace and the cathedral have been given over to community use.

Much is made too of cathedrals as spaces where people of all degrees of explicit allegiance or none may feel they belong. Yet there are limits to the use of this space. What place do flags and other military insignia, which sit so uneasily with the way of Christ, have in a Christian church? Services of remembrance can and should take place, but without 'religion hid in war', as Blake puts it.[12] Incarnation is a theological concept often used to support the open-minded and inclusive ministry of churches alongside all sorts and conditions of people. But incarnation does not mean baptising the *status quo* or accepting its values, for the coming of the Word into the world means judgement: 'The light has come into the world, but people preferred darkness to light because their deeds were evil' (John 3:19). Christian groups, with the spaces they inhabit, seek through God's grace to bear witness to the alternative culture of the Gospel: 'Among the Gentiles, kings lord it over their subjects; and those in authority are given the title

Benefactor. Not so with you: on the contrary, the greatest among you must bear themselves like the youngest, the one who rules like one who serves' (Luke 22:24f). Christians offer love and acceptance, seeking to embody that love and acceptance in which they have shared. They are part of a living temple, ministering to persons of flesh and blood with the human and financial resources at their disposal; only then do they turn to the care and preservation of bricks and mortar, glass and other artefacts.

~~~

Cathedrals have been transmitters of British culture, and as such have nurtured a much broader, open relationship between English society, culture and history on the one hand and the Church which bears witness to Christ on the other. A continuing problem for any cosmopolitan and non-dualistic ethos, incorporating the best from the culture of the surrounding society, is that it runs the risk of ending up in the same predicament as the wonderful edifice erected by Solomon, which opened up the puritanical religion of Yahweh to the richer, less austere culture of Canaan. The kings of the earth may bring their gifts into the new Jerusalem in repentance, yet their acceptance must be of the ways of God's justice for all, not of the privileges of the few. So I find myself among those whose concern is reflected in the following words from the recent report of the Archbishops' Commission on cathedrals: 'For some, both inside the Church and outside [the close affinity of cathedrals and private education] raises questions about the political or professional desirability of the Church being involved at all in independent [fee-paying] education'.[13] To which may be added a question of theological propriety too.

I agree with the sentiments of Blake's *Jerusalem* that cathedrals and churches may have a continuing part to play in

the religion of these islands. While it would be wrong to
ignore the attempts to play such a part, some of which are
described in this book, the shape of our medieval churches and
their distinctive ethos can make it difficult for them to be
responsive to the priorities of the Church's mission. Churches
have an ambivalent position in society, and as a result, like all
institutions, they have a continuous struggle to work out a
modus vivendi with contemporary culture. The civic role of
cathedrals demands even greater vigilance of their staff in the
maintenance of an alternative horizon within their life, their
preaching and their practical discipleship. My impression is
that the peculiar position of cathedrals has made it particularly
difficult for them to be countercultural signs. We now have an
opportunity to think again about mission and ways of bringing
the Gospel of Jesus Christ to our generation. Those of us who
use and are responsible for cathedrals, churches and chapels
should apply the Five Marks or Strands of Mission to our
buildings and their use, demanding as they are of human
and financial resources. These arose out of the 1988 Lambeth
Conference and were commended by the General Synod of the
Church of England to Anglican dioceses. They are: proclaiming
the good news of the Kingdom; teaching, baptising and nurturing new believers; responding to human need by loving
service; seeking to transform unjust structures of society;
striving to safeguard the integrity of creation and sustaining
and renewing the life of the earth. The role of our buildings
in fulfilling these tasks demands of us a theological, as well as
a purely pragmatic, answer.

Perhaps there is a way for the cathedrals to go on seeking
to work out a vision of service in liturgy and practical action.
According to the monastic ideal, buildings for divine worship,
living and service were alongside each other. So often in the
cathedrals of the 'new foundation' (that is, the old monastic
communities which became cathedrals at the Reformation), the
buildings which enabled service as a witness lie in ruins or have

been adopted for other purposes. They remain as a poignant testimony to a monastic ideal which has partly fallen into desuetude, and a challenge to us to recapture that balance between worship and action in the divine service. The devastation of monastic life in this country was a tragedy for British religion. Whatever may have been wrong with the monasteries in the sixteenth century, the wholesale destruction of a way of life in which worship and welfare were, in theory, closely intertwined, warts and all, is one of the less appealing parts of British social history. The remnants of those old monastic communities, which form the closes of many of our cathedrals, testify to that monastic ideal of divine service in the worship of lips and of lives, devoted in practical service, the latter being in no way inferior to the former.

In this essay I have echoed Blake's sympathetic description of the cathedrals as the 'friends of Albion', and his belief that they can be true friends in helping to point out and alleviate Albion's disease. I share Blake's hope that they will be beacons for our nation and a means of offering more than an aesthetic or vague religious experience. Jeremiah's stunning indictment of the Temple of the Lord and the complacent attitude of its supporters long ago, is a salutary reminder of the constant vigilance demanded of us as we seek to wrestle with the legacy of buildings and their contemporary use. Many will come into cathedrals echoing the disciples' wonder at 'the fine stones and ornaments' of the ancient Temple. Peter desired on the Mount of Transfiguration to build tabernacles to preserve or encapsulate the divine. Our need to create and maintain holy spaces is strong and its consequences far-reaching, but the glorious stones must never become an end in themselves. Christian institutions which seek to be true to the call of Jesus Christ must, as a first priority, respond to people who suffer hardship and dislocation, and who find themselves vulnerable or ignored. The risen Christ, the living Temple, is found (disconcertingly for most of us) in surprising and unprepossessing people, in a manner which is disturbing to a comfortable British Christian like myself. With whatever significance we, as humans, seek to endow Christian buildings, theologically they are no more deserving of attention as places where God may be found than, on the one hand, any place where two or three are gathered together, or on the other hand, than the persons of the poor, the outcast and the vulnerable. That will affect the way in which we view buildings, however grand and however venerable:

> The ugly, concrete block worship-space . . . can be a holy place, because it is occupied by and associated with a community of Christian people who are known, publicly known, for their acts of charity and peacemaking and who have drawn their building into the struggle for a radical openness to the will of God . . . To root the holiness of Christian sacred space in anything else is to be involved either in idolatry or in magic.[14]

Liturgy and service go hand in hand as parts of what constitutes the divine service, just as in the Torah, the service of the tabernacle went hand in hand with the practice of justice and mercy. All Christian communities must manifest that poverty of spirit which does not count worldly success as its sole criterion for devotion to Christ, is open to criticism, and is not sustained by self-righteousness. Where God is praised and reverenced and, in Ignatius of Loyola's words, no inordinate attachment is placed between oneself and God, a balance between tabernacle and social justice can be preserved. To be so attached to the sign is to be enslaved to the world of appearances, the world of the fallen senses. Many would see cathedrals as ways of opening the 'eternal worlds'. But too often a narrow aesthetic experience turns out to be no real opening to the eternal world, for it lacks encounters which produce the recognition that we cannot 'exist but by Brotherhood' (*Jerusalem* 96:28), and appropriate action to match.

I believe that Blake would have beckoned us to see the importance of the ambiguities of cathedrals as opportunities for imaginative creativity. The existence of what Blake describes as 'two contrary states' is not to be transcended with the result either that one dissolves into the other, or that one is in effect subordinated to the other. Rather, adequate attention is to be given to both poles, particularly the 'contrary' which we admire less and which most causes us discomfort. Cathedrals and holy places have become an established part of Christian culture; yet they do not fit easily with a theological tradition which is hardly warm in its support of sacred edifices, and which gives the central place to the nurture of 'living stones'. While we await that 'place where Contrarieties are equally true',[15] the tantalising and disconcerting effects of the contraries evident in cathedrals, churches and chapels can provoke us to be more vigilant for glimpses of Jerusalem in the midst of Babylon, and less complacent in our assumption that we know where these are to be found – for we will surely, to our surprise and consternation, find them in the least expected persons and places.

THREE

CATHEDRALS AND THEIR COMMUNITIES

NICOLAS ALLDRIT

COMMUNITY

The word 'community' has been much on our lips in recent decades. We speak of the European Community, community policing, community psychiatry, and the community of technologists. Not surprisingly there has been considerable interest in the concept; but the word has been applied to such a variety of human – and even vegetative – groupings that it is not easy to define; and as people often use the word in terms of what they think it ought to mean, or with a meaning subtly influenced by words from the same Latin root (commune, communal, communication, communism), discussion of the concept becomes very difficult.

In terms of etymology, anything can be called a community if its members have something in common. Thus in ecology the word is applied to plants sharing the same habitat; similarly, geographically, it denotes people living in the same town, village or neighbourhood. The lives of such a group of people *may* be interlocked by a complex of relationships; or, being at work all day, watching television in the evening, and going to bed at night, they may hardly know each other – and many of them may prefer such anonymity. One of them may call for greater 'community-mindedness'; but, desirable as it may be on various grounds that their lives should be more closely linked, this does not follow directly from their having a common habitat. Similarly, when we talk of a community of philatelists, we are defining them in terms of their common interest in stamps. No doubt some sort of *esprit de corps* develops between them, but it is the interest which they share that makes them a community.

That all those with any interest in a cathedral, from the dean to the most casual visitor, form a community of the widest kind is self-evident; and within this community, there are others – such as the regular worshippers, the flower arrangers, the guides, the vergers, the choir, and the residentiary canons – all of which can be defined in terms of their common task or interest. Some of the smaller groupings may develop bonds of fellow-feeling, though this is not inevitably so. However, another dimension is present, in that a cathedral is a place of Christian worship, and Christianity's definition of itself as a community involves the theology of what (in the original Greek of the New Testament) is called *koinonia*, a word which is usually translated as 'communion' or, less adequately, as 'fellowship'.

The idea behind *koinonia* is that Christians have certain spiritual realities in common. Not only do they share the good news of salvation; they share in Christ and in the grace which God the Father bestows through him; they share in Holy Communion; they share in the Holy Spirit; they share in the divine nature. Furthermore they share *with* Christ in his sufferings, death, burial, resurrection and exaltation, and they share with him in his relationship with the Father. Because they have these realities in common, Christians have *koinonia* with each other, and are bound together with each other and Christ, like the branches of a vine or the parts of a body. So in the Eucharist, Christians receive 'communion' not only in that they share in Christ, but also in that they share in each other. Constantly, in its exhortations to mutual love, the New Testament appeals to the common sharing in Christ and the gifts given through him. Christians are to love one another as Christ has loved them, and to wash each others' feet as Christ has washed theirs. All this makes the Church a community of a very special kind; and since the local church is a manifestation of the universal Church, what is true of the total Christian community, militant, expectant and triumphant, should be true of the particular body of Christians worshipping together at a particular place.

In the Acts of the Apostles St Luke gives us a picture of such a local church – that of Jerusalem – in the earliest years of Christianity.[1] The Jerusalem Christians were united in having one heart and one soul, and possessed everything in common. This picture has haunted the Church ever since, and this same picture was responsible for generating three models for a cathedral community: the semi-monastic canonical life, and the Augustinian and the Benedictine models. It also greatly influenced another – the prebendal model. We shall look at these in turn.

THE SEMI-MONASTIC CANONS

It has been suggested that some clergy came to be called *kanonikoi* or *canonici* because the word is a corruption of *koinonikoi*, so that the common life (and perhaps St Luke's picture of the Jerusalem church) is implicit in the word itself. More probably, however, a *canonicus* was a clergyman named in the *kanon* or list of the clergy of a particular church. Eusebius Vercellensis, who died in 370, seems to have introduced a system whereby such clergy, in what we would call a cathedral church, lived together, leading a semi-monastic life according to a Rule. Such a Rule was also called in Greek a *kanon*; this may have given an additional nuance to the word *canonicus*, which by the sixth century had become common currency in western Europe to denote a cathedral or collegiate clergyman. Pope Gelasius I (492–6) established *canonici regulares* in the Lateran palace, and the system whereby cathedral clergy lived a common life spread rapidly through Gaul, Spain and Africa. St Gregory the Great instructed St Augustine of Canterbury that in his see the bishop and clergy should live a common life together, similar to the monastic life in which St Augustine himself had been trained. These clergy were not monks, for those in minor orders were free to marry and live at home; but Gregory regarded such a system as following 'the way of life practised by our fathers at the beginning of the nascent church, who spoke of nothing as their personal property, but shared all things in common'[2] – a clear reference to Luke's picture of the early Jerusalem community in the Acts of the Apostles.

The bishop's *familia*

In about 750 Chrodegang, bishop of Metz, compiled a Rule for his own *familia* – the clergy who helped and advised him in administering his diocese – to order their common life. This was gradually adopted by other cathedrals, and in a modified form was imposed on the Frankish empire by the council of Aix-la-Chapelle in 816. The canons were to have a common dormitory and a common refectory, and were to reside in a close, where, however, each was allowed his own house. They were to leave the close only by the porter's gate. They had pastoral and liturgical duties, for which they could receive stipends. They could retain their own money and property, though these reverted to the community at their deaths.

This code was not without its influence in England. Two archbishops of Canterbury, Ethelheard and his successor Wulfred, gradually introduced it for their *familia*, the members of which seem to have possessed an Anglo-Saxon translation of the Rule, a copy of which is still extant. Leofric, the first bishop of Exeter, adopted it for his *familia* in 1050, as did

Gisa, bishop of Wells from 1061 to 1088. It disappeared, however, in the implementation of the Norman policy for cathedrals.

ST AUGUSTINE'S RULE

A second model for cathedral community life which owed much to Luke's picture of the early Jerusalem church was created by St Augustine of Hippo, who, when he became the sole bishop of Hippo in 396, formed his *familia* into a monastery. Following earlier forms of monasticism of which Augustine was aware, this was to be a contemplative community – though unlike them it encouraged the study of books and intellectual conversation. But since its members had responsibilities towards the diocese, it inevitably became a 'mixed' or even an 'active' form of monasticism. After the Lateran synod of 1059 had exhorted cathedral clergy to live together, to hold all things in common, and to lead 'the apostolic life', after the example of the early Jerusalem church, Augustine's pattern became popular. Chrodegang's Rule had proved too difficult for secular clergy, and it was continually being relaxed and unsuccessfully restored. It was now felt that an active monastic pattern would work better. St Peter Damian taught that the call to a fully communal life was scriptural and obligatory on all clergy for whom it was possible. It was a matter of 'imitating the tender babyhood of the church still at the breast'. The Gregorian Reform (whose leading figure was Hildebrand, who became Pope Gregory VII in 1073) saw this as a way of getting rid of simony, clerical marriage and concubinage.

The need was therefore felt for an appropriate Rule. It was found in 'the Rule of St Augustine' – actually a collection of documents of varying provenance and existing in several different forms, but including Augustine's Epistle 211, which is probably a summary of instructions given orally to his community and read to them once a week in order to keep their ideals before their minds. For this reason it is more concerned with principles than with details, and this may have been a reason for its success when it was rediscovered in the eleventh century. A community following the Rule was Augustinian in spirit; it could create its own 'customary' to specify the details of how the ideals were to be implemented.

Augustine's ideal was that of the early Jerusalem church – as shown by his reaction to one of his clergy who, like Ananias, had retained some property. Two of his surviving sermons refer to the matter: the second was preceded by Augustine taking the book of the Acts of the Apostles from his lector and reading out the passage about the apostolic way of life. The same passage is the basis of his Epistle 211. The monks are to be of 'one heart and mind on the road to God', for they have come together for brotherly love. They are to honour God in one another, to respect the uniqueness of each member of the community and value his gifts, and to be concerned for the interests of the community as a whole. The community's life requires fixed times for corporate prayer, and the words uttered by the lips should be alive in the heart. Advice is given about food and clothing, care of the sick, and coping with conflict – and warnings to those at fault. Each member of the community is to be responsible for the others, though the provost has a special task in the concluding phases of some processes. He is to be respected not because he is at the top of a hierarchy, but because he is at the base of the community.

In England, the Norman conquest occurred just before the Rule of St Augustine had become general in the Continental cathedrals. But because of its flexibility and its intention to provide for active work outside the community, the Rule proved useful for groups of clergy engaged in activities other than the diocesan or parochial, such as looking after a hospital. Even some contemplative communities adopted the Rule. Thus a large number of Augustinian communities (which were not cathedrals) came into existence in England. One of them was founded in Carlisle, a city recently restored after the Danish depredations in 1102. Henry I made it the see of a bishop in 1133.

BENEDICTINE MONASTICISM

A third model for cathedral life was based on the Rule of St Benedict. Much has been written about Benedictine monasticism which it is unnecessary to repeat here. Suffice it to say that Benedict, probably a layman, never envisaged having a bishop's cathedra in one of his monasteries; and even though Augustine's Epistle 211 was one of the sources of his Rule, he did not, as Augustine did, envisage his monks working outside the monastery. Though 'guests are never lacking in a monastery', it does not exist for their sake, but for the monks, that they 'may by a straight course reach our Creator' – and even the communal life of the monastery is subordinate to this aim. All this makes it surprising that a bishop's *familia* should be a Benedictine community – a phenomenon largely confined to England.

This is not to say that monasticism derived from much the same contemplative traditions as Benedict's was never involved in the administration of the surrounding district. The Celtic Church was structured on a tribal and monastic basis whereby the abbot of the monastery, who was usually a priest, managed the local churches, while the bishop was a simple monk who exercised his episcopal sacramental functions at the abbot's direction, with no more say in the monastery, or in the district, than any other monk. This was the original system in Lindisfarne, Hexham, Iona and other northern sees; but Bede in his time called this 'an unaccustomed arrangement'. By the ninth century, monastic life had in any case nearly died out in England, and it was as part of the tenth-century movement towards its restoration, led by St Dunstan and supported by various kings, that Benedictine cathedrals came into being – the first being Winchester, where St Ethelwold, the bishop in 963, replaced the secular canons with Benedictine monks from Abingdon, under a prior, with the bishop as titular abbot. Worcester followed in 974, and Sherborne in 978. In each case, the bishop was a monk seeking to improve the spirituality of the cathedral clergy.

After the Conquest this arrangement appealed to the Normans, and it was adopted by Rochester (1082), Durham (1093), Norwich (1096) and Ely (1109). In 1088 the see of Wells, which had a secular chapter, was moved to Bath abbey, and in 1095 custody of the abbey of Coventry was granted to the bishop of Chester, who transferred his see to it. From a liturgical point of view it was undoubtedly a better arrangement than the prebendal system (apart from Carlisle, this was the only alternative tolerated by the Normans), for all the members kept perpetual residence; this also gave them a deeper sense of *koinonia*. On the principle that no news is good news, we may assume that most of the time, in most places, these advantages balanced the disadvantages.

But disadvantages there were, because of the inevitable tension between the Benedictine ideal and the episcopal task. At times this tension erupted into bitter conflict. The bishop's time was largely taken up with administration of the diocese, which could be enormous, and increasingly he became involved in secular affairs as, in effect, a royal minister and diplomat, so that episcopal functions had to be performed by suffragans. The bishop needed clerical assistants, diocesan administrators and canonists to a greater extent than ever before. But the community of monks might not include any people suitable for such tasks. Had there been such people, then the community might in any case have regarded them as extraneous to the Benedictine life. A Benedictine community could not be the bishop's *familia* in any real sense, and the bishop commonly formed his real *familia* outside the community. In 1189

Bishop Hugh de Nonant drove the monks out of Coventry, replacing them with secular canons, and warning the king, 'In two months, believe me, there shall be no monk in any bishop's church in your kingdom, for it isn't right. The monks can go to the devil.'[3]

It is significant that the long conflict between the archbishops and monks of Canterbury began when Archbishop Baldwin proposed to found a college of secular canons, probably for his own administrative clerks; inevitably the monks suspected that the final result would be the transfer to the college, if not of the see, at least of their power of election. For these problems were exacerbated by the loss of the balance which Benedict incorporated in his Rule. This required that the abbot, who is to be obeyed 'as if the command came from God himself', should be elected by the monks, and that the abbot should appoint the prior. But in the cathedral abbey, the abbot was a bishop, who might be a Crown nominee over whose appointment they might have no effective control. Even if he were a monk, he might not be a member of their own community whom they had come to love and respect. He might not in any case be the sort of monk they would ever have elected to the abbacy. He might not be a monk at all, and be ignorant of, or unsympathetic to, the Benedictine life. But the bishop still claimed the right to elect the monks' prior (at least until the monks won this right, after many years of conflict), and to interfere in their life in other ways, even though he might be away on business much of the time and live in a separate palace. One chronicler wrote: 'It was natural and customary for the monks of Rochester to annoy and slander their well-deserving bishops, who were always compelled to have a staff ready to defend themselves against the monks'.[4]

THE PREBENDAL MODEL

The fourth cathedral model was the prebendal system. In an organised form, this can be traced back to shortly after 1070, when Lanfranc became archbishop of Canterbury. At this time, constitutions of the English cathedral, hitherto largely unwritten, began to be revised and formulated. Those which were not Benedictine or Augustinian were set up with deans, precentors, chancellors and treasurers, on a prebendal plan. Such were Chichester, Exeter, Hereford, Lichfield, Lincoln, London, Salisbury, Wells and York. This system resulted from a long development, for bishops in the early Church had often granted land or a vineyard to a member of the *familia* as a kind of stipend. In the ninth century this further developed as an alternative to the canonical life. Its acceptance as a legitimate development caused the reaction that, along with other factors, resulted in the Augustinian movement.

A prebendal cathedral was largely supported by gifts of land or money, which in the beginning were made to the bishop. Sometimes they were made specifically for the prebend, or income, of a canon. The bishop kept some of the revenues for himself; some went into the cathedral's Common Fund; the rest was divided among the canons so that each received his prebend or separate income. These canons formed the chapter which elected the bishop. They were bound by no vows except those of their ordination; there were, however, statutes which controlled their behaviour and their administration of the cathedral. They had houses in the close (a survival from Chrodegang's semi-monastic enclosure), but for much of the time they did not live in them. They paid vicars to fulfil their duties in the cathedral, and, living on the remainder of their income, they resided in country parishes part of the year, or fulfilled duties in universities or at court. Some were appointed to their canonries by papal decree, simply to provide them with an income while engaged in the pope's business. J. W. Parker gives some statistics of residence (drawn from the Lincoln rolls *Recedendi et Veniendi*, i.e. of the goings and comings of the canons): 'In 1278/9 [the roll] showed that during a period of 15 weeks, 29 out of 52 canons were entered on the roll as resident, and 20 of them kept more than a couple of weeks' residence.' In the fourteenth century the number of canons in residence at a time once dropped 'as low as seven, and in five of the years it was as many as 15'.

In this system, almost as much as in the monastic, the idea of cathedral clergy as the bishop's *familia* was breaking down, though individual canons might be employed by the bishop in diocesan administration. Furthermore, it was impossible for canons to lead a common life in a monastic or semi-monastic sense. Nevertheless, there were still traces of monasticism. The divine office, though not celebrated according to the Benedictine rite, was still of the monastic type, based on the singing of the Psalter in course throughout the week and the continuous reading of Scripture. This had, of course, been true of all churches since the seventh century, but few other than cathedrals and collegiate churches could sing the whole office chorally and with due ceremonial. Though the canons were not living the common life, the vicars were – although they do not seem always to have been more committed to it than they could help. The Lincoln *Statuta Vicariorum* and the provisions for them in the *Novum Registrum* seem to be based on principles similar to those that Chrodegang had set out for canons. It was almost as if the vicars deputised for the canons in their community, as well as in their liturgical functions. If they misbehaved in a schoolboyish way (as they often did), they were liable to find themselves in trouble on the following Saturday morning, when they would be reprimanded or punished according to a pattern that was clearly based on the monastic Chapter of Faults. The daily chapter office after Prime, with spiritual reading, was also an imitation of Benedictine practice, as was the collation, a light meal accompanied by spiritual reading between Evensong and Compline in Lent.

Apart from these monastic elements, a sense of brotherhood was further expressed in the practice of taking food and drink together. That invitations to luncheon were given by a clerk in choir dress during the Te Deum at Matins and during the gradual at High Mass, 'according to ancient custom', as the Lincoln statute stated, shows that this meal was regarded as theologically significant. So too were the loving-cups, drunk at Salisbury during the singing of the gospel[6] on Maundy Thursday by everybody from the bishop down to the sacristan's assistants. The precise amount of drink was specified: for example, the succentor had one *lagena* of wine and one of ale, and each chorister had a *potellum* of wine and one of ale. (Latham's *Mediaeval Latin Word-list* translates *lagena* as a gallon and *potellum* as a quart.) One hopes they took some of it home for other occasions, but much conviviality must have been fostered. At the words at the end of the gospel – 'Arise, let us go hence' – they were to depart 'peacefully, with thanksgiving'. Some cathedral chapters were also made communities of prayer by the division of the Psalter between the canons. In addition to the office, they were to recite a portion of the Psalter, whether they were in residence or not. This practice has been adopted by some more recently founded cathedrals, including Southwell and Truro.

THE PLACE OF THE LAITY

Of these four models, the only one to survive the Reformation was the prebendal, and even this was significantly transformed. As with the other models, the underlying pre-Reformation assumption was that the chapter, along with the vicars, other clerics, and choirboys, were themselves identified as the cathedral's worshipping community. Others were expected to worship in parish churches. That there were, nevertheless, people who attended cathedral worship is implied by the intercessory prayers ('Bidding of the Bedes'), which in the cathedrals of the Old Foundation were said in the procession before high Mass on all Sundays except Palm Sunday. These, or at least the biddings addressed to the people, were in English, and in some places a sermon in English was added. There was little other liturgical recognition of the presence of a congregation. The professionals within a cathedral were neither leading nor inspiring a congregation, but simply worshipping, each by fulfilling his own task.

The Reformation, however, emphasised 'edification' of the people, and even though the people may not have participated vocally much more than before, when they were present they were regarded as an integral part of the worshipping community. This made the cathedral, in principle, much more like a parish church. Two further developments have enlarged the role of the laity: first, some parish churches have become cathedrals (while retaining something of their former character); and secondly, church music has developed to the point where lay singers are needed. Taken together, these three factors mean that the worshipping body of a cathedral comprises mainly laity – and thus the cathedral is like the whole Church of God of which it is an earthly manifestation.

In many cathedrals which are not also parish churches, the implications of this important post-Reformation development need to be more fully realised, for little power is allowed to the laity in cathedral statutes. It is recognised, particularly in view of the emphasis on the role of the laity in the Church in recent theology, that there is a need to move forward on this matter. But the difficulty is that all four previous cathedral models were essentially clerical. This has an important bearing on the question of the viability of a return to any of the models in cathedrals of the present or future. Apart from the theological issue, any such return would undercut many of the developments connected with the post-Reformation role of the laity, such as the maintenance of the rich heritage of cathedral music.

FUTURE PATTERNS

Any consideration of the future of cathedrals needs to reflect seriously on the possibility of a return to their original function, whereby the cathedral clergy were the bishop's *familia*. But it was precisely this function which, as we have seen, proved so difficult to reconcile with the Benedictine model. Although Benedictine communities vary considerably nowadays as to the degree of their involvement with the world, there is a tendency for them to look back to the intentions of their founder, and any movement in that direction would be likely to conflict with the movement back to being the bishop's *familia*. A broadly Augustinian or semi-monastic model might seem more compatible with such a return, but even here there would be practical difficulties, not least the fact that the most able person to fulfil a particular role in the *familia* might be married.

We have seen that each of the models did not always work well in its own day, and we may well wonder whether Luke's picture of the early Jerusalem church, on which the models depended to varying degrees, has not haunted cathedrals rather too much. Probably Luke intended his model to be descriptive rather than prescriptive – and even as descriptive it may have been somewhat idealised, for his language seems to have been influenced by two Greek maxims which Aristotle quoted,[7] and by stock descriptions of the Pythagorean way of life; he may have been describing early Christian almsgiving (called *koinonia* in Hebrews 13:16) in such a way as to suggest the fulfilment of the Greek ideal. Paul assumed that it was legitimate for Christians to hold private property, and the fact that he needed to organise the collection for the Jerusalem church suggests that, if that church had had a communistic system, the system had broken down.

Valuable as Luke's picture has been in helping the development of monasticism, it is not obvious that it has direct relevance to cathedrals. Rather, cathedrals like other Christian communities should be informed by the broader teaching on *koinonia* to be found in the New Testament and in the Christian tradition. Thus cathedrals which have not worked with the bishop in terms of the *familia* model, have the challenge issued by the tradition to do so. Where some of the bishop's staff are also canons of the cathedral, such an exploration might be particularly fruitful.

The monastic tradition in its various forms is also a quarry in which may be discovered appropriate models of community for today. Those who live in the vicinity of cathedrals should consider adopting some form of 'rule', which would include common worship and prayer, meeting together to discuss matters of common concern, and mutual pastoral care. Such a pattern is not monastic, but recent writings have indicated how the Rule of St Benedict, for example, might be applied to clergy and laity alike today.[8] Then the life of a cathedral community will extend to care for others who are not of that immediate circle – as monastic life did in the past and does in the present. Some cathedrals already support within their bounds Abbeyfield homes for the elderly, and small communities (or other provision) for the care of those who have found themselves to be casualties of contemporary life. The embracing of L'Arche communities for the disabled may be another possible model to develop. The broader New Testament teaching on *koinonia* suggests a pattern that reaches out and cares for the wider community, and in so doing proclaims the coming Kingdom of God. It is a model of the Church that looks outwards, rather than inwards into a self-contained community bound by the needs of the cathedral itself.

FOUR

WALKING IN PATTERNS

Cathedral worship

DAVID STANCLIFFE

'Now I know why the churches are true', said a four year old, watching a televised service from one of our cathedrals. 'The people in them enjoy singing, and walk about in patterns.'

The reason why that comment has always rung true for me is that the four year old instinctively grasped that worship has to do with celebrating, and holding together the apparent contradiction of spontaneity and order. In worship we bring the raw energy of our passionate desire to reach out beyond the limits of our own vision into a place where it can be ordered, interpreted and offered as a vehicle for the transformation of people and communities alike. To paraphrase that child's words, cathedrals are true because they make and celebrate liturgy. It is in ordered acts of worship which catch fire that we are drawn into that transforming relationship with God. But liturgical worship is not the only context in which this happens: the buildings themselves, even when no actual service is taking place, embody something of that dynamic of transformation, as does the community which gathers round them and is shaped by them.

By liturgy, therefore, I do not only mean particular services, but the whole process of making visible in a building, in its worship and in its community a style of corporate life into which people can be drawn. This process is rooted in the particularity of who and how we are, and any one act of worship offers us a snapshot of that particular community's life at that moment; worship must have an incarnational root. But worship is not only about expressing who and how we are: it is also about catching us up into the continuous process of redemptive change which is part of God's continuing activity of transforming not only us as individuals but also his whole world. A particular act of worship cannot therefore be divorced from its roots in the community which celebrates, or from that community's particular vision of what God would have it be. Every liturgy relates both to the incarnation and to the redemptive work of Christ, so those who create and celebrate liturgies need to be aware of which community they are working with, and of its particular vision of transformation. No one liturgy can do everything for everyone on every occasion, and a particular opportunity open to cathedrals is to develop a number of styles in response to the variety of communities with which they are working.

For this reason it is important, in planning any particular liturgy, to recognise which mode of 'being cathedral' is foremost. This may seem a rather bold, and perhaps partisan, claim. Let me begin further back. From the point of view of the outsider, cathedrals frequently seem inaccessible and mysterious – characteristics which are reflected in their worship. In trying to make sense of what goes on in cathedral worship, people start to analyse the ways in which it is different from their own experience. They come to a service, and find that there is little opportunity for active participation: the musical as well as the architectural idiom is worlds away from what they know as church. It is all too easy for these experiences to be written up into a post-Barchester mythology which says that cathedrals are locked in their own world, and understand neither the rest of the Church nor the culture in which they are set.

My experience is that this is the reverse of the truth, and that cathedrals struggle hard to work with the various registers demanded of them. Giving liturgical expression to such celebrations in a way that engages with people and also offers a process of transformation demands integrity as well as theological and liturgical acumen. In contrast to parish churches, cathedrals have considerable resources and fewer constraints. People expect cathedrals to offer a range of liturgical worship and a diversity of style which would not be tolerated by a regular parish congregation. At the same time, cathedrals which offer everything to everyone can thereby easily fall into the trap of losing their own identity and integrity. So how do cathedrals establish both their community and their liturgical identity with equal integrity and clarity? What ecclesiology or model of the Church undergirds that identity? How do we match this integrity with the expressed hopes and desires of those who want to articulate their sense that life is a gift, and to offer the best they can in response?

What we meet in a cathedral, at first glance, are two visible realities coexisting uneasily. First, there is the cathedral building, giving visible expression to a major historical institution, with its structured life enshrined in statutes and expressed in a traditional liturgy celebrated by a hierarchy of clergy and choir. The second reality is the enormous variety of people who come to the cathedral. They range from uncomprehending tourists, through the curious and enquiring, to the informed and devout from all walks of life and of all ages and nationalities. This variety is expressed in the large range of purposes for which the cathedral is used liturgically and semi-liturgically. There are concerts, plays and community operas which bring crowds into a cathedral for an experience which is often para-liturgical – an experience of engagement and transformation in its widest sense. There are children's workshops and youth festivals; there are lectures and dialogues on a variety of important subjects under the broad heading of social and moral concern; there are services for the celebration of civic life, often focused on the work of particular charities; there are services occasioned by one-off events which, locally or nationally, have touched the community's heart – like the Dunblane massacre or the Hillsborough disaster, or the unveiling of the Prisoners of Conscience window or the Rio de Janeiro world summit; there are diocesan celebrations like the regular ordinations, the celebration of the ministry of healing, the centenary of the founding of the diocese or the installation of a new bishop; there are the regular celebrations of the liturgical year, from the Advent carol procession through the celebration of Holy Week and Easter to the cathedral festival; there is the regular Sunday celebration of the Eucharist, with its gathered congregation; there is the daily prayer – said or sung – of the core community with its attendant eavesdroppers. All these make up the complex diet of the cathedral's liturgical life – or do they? Making such a list of what goes on raises the question as to whether cathedrals are just institutions which provide an umbrella under which a whole host of different activities take place – a building and resources which can be hired out to all comers – or whether cathedrals consciously embrace and own these different activities as manifestations of their multifarious, but ultimately coherent, life.

In his book *Models of the Church*, Avery Dulles analyses vividly a number of different ways in which the Church understands itself.[1] The chapter headings are indicative of the author's background (an American Jesuit) and of his particular concern to help the Church understand the different ways in which it understands itself for particular purposes Beginning with 'The Church as institution', he moves to 'The Church as mystical communion', 'The Church as sacrament', 'The Church as herald' and 'The Church as servant'. To each of these paradigms he attaches one or more biblical models or traditional concepts, and makes some analysis of the strengths and weaknesses of each. What is the Church's self-understanding of its place in the tradition, in the human community and in relation to the purposes of God? His analysis has been both helpful and influential. This chapter attempts a parallel exercise to that of Avery Dulles: it looks at some of the current models of cathedral. And asks what style of 'being Church' they are adopting (consciously or otherwise) and what kind of liturgy might be appropriate to each model. The models include cathedral as institution; cathedral as community – the body of Christ; cathedral as community – the people of God; cathedral as gathered congregation; cathedral as the bishop's church – a sacramental centre of unity; and the cathedral as herald and prophet. What follows is not a slavish attempt to fit the different and complex ways of 'being cathedral' into the Dulles mould, but a number of worked examples about how a particular community's theological self-understanding on a particular occasion can help shape an appropriate liturgy and the way in which it is celebrated.

CATHEDRAL AS INSTITUTION

Many people experience cathedrals primarily as institutions. Cathedrals are synonymous with great buildings, and often own other property besides. Some of them have considerable wealth, and an annual turnover equal to, or sometimes in excess of, that of the diocese as a whole. Older cathedrals were founded, or refounded, by Henry VIII largely on the model of Oxbridge colleges. They were to provide a common room of learning gathered around common prayer, a common table and a library. They were the successors of the Benedictine cathedrals of the Middle Ages, and their institutional indepen-

dence from the bishop and the diocese reflects this. The ideals
of this common life are enshrined in statutes, which frequently
reflect – as the safety net of legal formularies needs to – how
to manage an institution when there is friction or division,
rather than modelling the ideals of good practice. Clarity about
the statutory responsibilities of those who lead the cathedral's
life, and the establishment of an ordered hierarchy of decision-
making, infiltrates its liturgical life. Statutes lay down who
orders the liturgy, who may preside at the Eucharist on which
occasions, who may read, and who may preach – and this
means that in some cathedrals even today the style of liturgical
life varies from month to month, depending on which canon
is 'in residence'. This is hardly a recipe for sustaining common
prayer and common life! And it has other effects too. In some
places, regardless of who is presiding at the liturgy, members
of the chapter walk in procession in order of seniority. What
model of collegiate or sacramental life is presented when such
matters are always determined by hierarchy and precedence,
rather than by role or function?

Institutionally, the ambivalence about whose cathedral it is
means that the bishop is sometimes treated more as the Visitor
than as the diocesan bishop; if he finds himself welcomed to
his cathedral, or even described as the bishop of X, as if he
were a visitor from another diocese, little wonder that there is
sometimes confusion over his liturgical role. This institutional
unclarity may lead some bishops unconsciously to avoid their
cathedrals, except on those occasions like Christmas and Easter
when their responsibilities are enshrined in statute and everyone's expectations are clear.

Liturgies which model the institutional life are an essential
part of the cathedral's liturgical fabric. Perhaps most typical
would be the installation of a bishop or dean, when the liturgy
customarily inducts the new arrival into the various layers of
their new responsibilities. The cathedral, the close, the city,
the diocese – these layers of Church and state are carefully

interleaved, and appropriate and symbolic objects are produced (and often laboriously explained) at each stage as the liturgy moves from the door (the threshold with the outside world), into the body of the nave (the place of the people), and from there into the choir (the place where the collegiate life of the cathedral is embodied), to the principal altar (where the sacraments are focused). Such services reinforce and teach a good deal about the hierarchy of the institution, but they do not always sit easily with the proclamation of the Gospel of a God who comes among his people in the form of a servant, who steps over thresholds between sacred and secular with a sharp eye for truth and humbug, and who teaches people that holiness is as likely to be experienced in a community of love as in the meticulously nuanced patterns of hierarchical order, however carefully they are crafted to reflect in human terms something of the order of God's new creation.

None the less, the institutional life of the Church is important. It gives visibility and structure to the manifestation of Christ's life in word and sacrament. It emphasises the continuity of the tradition – with the medieval theocratic vision if not with the simplicities of the apostolic age. But where the institution takes on a life of its own and is no longer subject to that perpetual recalling to transformation, good liturgy will be difficult to devise. Hierarchical and institutional patterns, and the statutes that enshrine them, may need adapting when they are inimical to theologically unsustainable practices.

THE CATHEDRAL AS COMMUNITY

The second model – and one with many layers – is of the cathedral as community. To describe the cathedral as community is perhaps as obvious as talking of the cathedral as institution, but it is more complex. Every group or association of people likes to describe themselves as community, and cathedrals are no exception. But which community is the cathedral? Is it those who are named in the statutes or hold office in the organisation? Is it those who live in the close? Is it those who regularly worship there – and do we mean daily, weekly or annually, when the Greater Chapter meets? Cathedral communities are many-layered, and people may belong in more than one. None the less, unless we are clear which layer or community we are talking about, questions about how the community gathers, what liturgy and language it uses to offer its worship and express itself, who presides and what liturgical style is appropriate, will be difficult to resolve.

At the root of the model of cathedral as community is the English attachment to the Benedictine style with its emphasis on a common life centred on stability, on ordered worship and on intellectual vigour. These are high ideals, and part of our commitment to them is about being physically present. If the choir is always touring Australia or making recordings, then the sense of *stabilitas* is threatened. If the canons and others only attend worship when they feel like it or are on the rota to lead it (what does 'in residence' mean, or imply, about those who are not?), then there will be little real commitment to common prayer: the cathedral's life will not model community, but cost-effective functionality. If members of the chapter do not hear each other preach and so let their preaching be shaped by what they learn from one another, then their hearers will only hear a series of disconnected 'occasional sermons', rather than being drawn into a community of thought, an interwoven tapestry of minds which are being stretched beyond where they would naturally reach on their own. Excellence is achieved not by individual brilliance, but by a visible complementarity of skills which reveals the unity of the Church as the body of Christ, and where that unity in diversity is clearly relished by its participants.

Cathedral as community: the body of Christ

Behind the model of the cathedral as community lies the Pauline model of the Church as the body of Christ. That model – so exalted by the church builders and the liturgists of the 1960s and 1970s – has indeed much to offer, but its exclusive predominance has its hazards. For all its organic overtones, the eucharistic theology developed from this model – visible in Rite A in the Alternative Service Book 1980, and the architectural forms in which that theology is expressed – typically in Sir Frederick Gibberd's circular Metropolitan Cathedral of Christ the King in Liverpool – manage to convey a static quality. In a circular building where all face the centre there is only one focus, only one place to put the altar. But the powerful central focus has its drawbacks. From where do you preach the word? Where do you start your journey, and place the font? What leads you on in your journey, when you can see everything from the entrance? Where else is there to go? And in terms of eucharistic theology, the same is true. Drawn into union in the body of Christ, why should you ever go anywhere else? With such a strongly inward-looking focus, what will turn you outwards? What will break the charmed circle, the cosy club gathered round the table, and make the Church recover its sense of mission in the way it expresses its liturgical life?

At the heart of this community model is a sense of ingathering. An incarnational theology models for us the discovery of God in our midst, into whose life we are drawn. The Benedictine tradition has at its heart the practice of hospitality. The stranger must be received as Christ himself: we are drawn into the community's life, enfolded in love. But at the centre of the community's life is a stillness, a waiting on God. Corporate silent prayer is very powerful, as is the low murmur of those who gather in the early morning to pray the psalms. The way in which the Psalter is recited corporately is the most telling indicator of the quality of a community's life, and how the liturgy is prayed. Are they competing with each other to lead, are they keeping their voices down to a level where they can hear their neighbours more easily than themselves, or are they centred on God? This gathered concentration, providing a moment of great stillness, is also what remains quintessentially Anglican about cathedral Evensong. What draws people to cathedral Evensong? I believe that it is the chance of being, for 40 minutes or so – outsider though you may be – a member of that community at prayer. That is why sinking into a stall in choir is so different from sitting on a chair in the front row of the nave. In cathedrals too, as in other communities, there are insiders and outsiders, and we long to be insiders – 'Nearer, my God, to Thee' – and to be drawn into an eternal rhythm of praise and intercession, the twin poles of daily prayer.

Cathedral as community: the people of God
But the religious life is also a journey; a journey into God, a journey in the pursuit of truth. Alongside the image of the body of Christ lies the image of the people of God. That is why it is always appropriate to ask of those who claim the banner of community such questions as, 'Where are you going? How are you growing? For whose sake do you exist?' As well as stability, there is momentum; as well as cathedral liturgies which gather the community, there are those which take us on a journey. These two elements – expressed architecturally in the circular and the linear – find their theological anchor in incarnation and in redemption, the two key moments of God's encounter with his people which any liturgy worth its salt needs to embody in the experience it offers.[2]

Many of our cathedrals were designed primarily as processional spaces in which pilgrimage might be made. This is not just true of those which held the shrines of much-venerated saints; the elaborate processions before the principal Mass of Sunday in cathedrals like Salisbury had an important symbolic significance which we cannot easily appreciate.[3] We are used to cathedral naves full of chairs and to congregations turned into audiences, where each person has a seat and stays there, watching the professionals on stage. But when the whole assembly moves through the building, then the sense that the Church, the whole people of God, is on a pilgrimage journey is powerfully enacted.

No liturgy so clearly reinforces this image as that of the Easter Vigil. In Salisbury, for example, candidates for baptism huddle round the cloisters where, next to the well-head, the bonfire burns. By the light of this camp-fire the songs of deliverance are sung and the old stories rehearsed – the creation, Noah's ark, Abraham and Isaac; the burning bush, the Passover and the Exodus; Daniel in the lions' den, the burning fiery furnace, Jonah in the belly of the great fish, the valley of the dry bones and others.[4] Then, with a single fragile light, the company moves into the vast, cold, tomb-like interior of the cathedral, where the flickering light on the ribs of the vault makes you feel swallowed up in the skeletal belly of this great monster. And when the company has penetrated into the heart of the darkness, then the resurrection is proclaimed, and with a great shout the darkness is destroyed. The gongs and trumpets drown the organ, and the candidates go down into the cold water of death only to be raised to new life with the risen Christ in the first light of dawn, as, clothed and anointed, they move forward to share in the breaking of the bread as the night breaks into day.

That processional movement rehearses the journey each of us is called to make daily – even hourly – in our dying to sin and rising to new life, annually in our celebration of the liturgical year, and throughout our lifetime as we move always closer to our own death. It is a journey we do not make alone. We make it in the company of our fellow travellers, those who belong now in the life of the Church world-wide, and with the saints of every age who have trodden this way before us.

And where is the journey going? The easy answer is that it

is going to God. We have many hymns which rehearse the golden glories of heaven, and our liturgies tend to end up with people gathered – or looking towards – a distant altar in the east from which God's blessing is pronounced. Being drawn into the life of the holy Trinity, to share the heavenly banquet, is the ultimate model of community in most people's minds. And yet where is God to be found? Is he not in his world, in the pinched faces of the hungry and homeless, in the battered, the rejected, the lonely, the poor? In the Eucharist (Rite A), the final section, titled 'The Dismissal', contains what is probably the most disobeyed rubric: *'The ministers and people depart'*. In the liturgy we need a way of helping people not to be so seduced by the promise of heaven that they cannot engage with what God is doing in the world now. This implies identifying with a theology of community wider than that of cathedral. Our dismissal rites need as much theological scrutiny as our gathering rites, and have a lot to teach us about our theology of mission. In all these cathedral rites, whether emphasising the incarnational focus in our midst or the dynamic movement of the sacramental rites – initiation, ordination, reconciliation and healing or Eucharist – there is a distinct model of community. In one, especially in the daily celebration of the offices of Morning and Evening Prayer, there is a pattern of in-gathering; in the other, the sacramental mode, there is a dynamic of change as people step across the threshold from one stage of their journey to the next. In one, the gathered community's liturgical prayer is 'monastic' in style, a model of focused stillness; in the other, the successor to the 'cathedral office' of the early Church,[5] a more light-footed approach values a simpler pattern of daily prayer, with more repetitive chant and movement. It is from this tradition that extended vigil rites, like the popular Advent carol processions, have developed. This pattern contrasts with the monastic-style prayer of the 'professional Christians', reading the whole Psalter and the Bible in course.

One of the distinctive features of the English cathedral tradition is that these complementary emphases coexist so fruitfully. The over-dominance of one or the other would not only lead to a theological imbalance between the incarnation and the redemption, but also to models where episcopal dominance or capitular independence would threaten the delicately balanced partnership which, at their best, our cathedrals embody.

CATHEDRAL AS GATHERED CONGREGATION

Questions about the layers of community, and the location of the focus of each, also raise questions about the congregation. Very often 'congregation' means the worshippers who choose to gather for their Sunday morning worship in the cathedral rather than in their local parish church, and who are drawn to the cathedral for a variety of reasons, including liturgical style, music, preaching – and not infrequently because of their desire to escape the demands of a local parish and its needs.

From the cathedral's perspective, having a congregation is a not unwelcome opportunity. It fits the current orthodoxy that the life of the Church is exhibited primarily in gathered congregations in parishes. There are a number of cathedrals whose senior clergy have been formed in the larger parish churches, and who bring with them to the ministry of a cathedral their longing for a regular congregation, meeting together week by week at the Sunday Eucharist. Deans and provosts tend to bring a sense that their primary relationships and responsibilities are to and for 'their' congregation. In a number of places, this has produced a shift in the liturgical style towards the 'parish communionisation' of the principal Sunday Eucharist. Who should preside at the liturgy, and who should preach? Should there be consistency in preaching, or courses? How do we nurture the faith of our congregation? May we question the place in the tradition of the longer musical settings? Is the presentation of the Eucharist excessively clerical? All these questions have in many ways been a welcome reaction to, and development from, the more detached and unquestioning assumption that the cathedral is primarily an institution, where the actual worshippers have – at any rate in the statutes of older cathedrals – neither place nor voice.

But there are dangers here. Is the cathedral doing more than modelling the parish church writ large, if nothing distinctive of a cathedral is being shown in the liturgy and the way in which it is celebrated? If it is not clear from the style of celebration either that it is the bishop's church, and the place where the ministry of the whole diocese is focused, or that it is the church of a community, charged with modelling a distinctive style of collaboration and trust, then something essential is missing.

What, then, can the model of the cathedral as congregation deliver? Should it not be a visible expression of the church that congregates, which is called together from the parishes to model in miniature the life of the diocese as a whole? Should it not be a congregation where the unity of the Church, made up of so many different strands, rather than solid uniformity, is made visible? Is not this the point of a congregation that is shaped not by locality and geography, nor yet by distinctive or exclusive theologies or churchmanship, but by a desire to model the Church in all its fullness? Perhaps this is why the Pauline model of the church as the body of Christ, with its sense of a single organic community, seems to fit less easily in relation to cathedrals. The gathering of the congregation for the principal Eucharist on Sunday is more open-ended and multilayered than that. Sunday morning congregations in cathedrals – even though the Parish Communion Movement's influence is strong – always include visitors of one sort or another, and the distinct layers of the cathedral's various communities are nearly always visible.

THE CATHEDRAL AS THE BISHOP'S CHURCH:
SACRAMENTAL UNITY

This visibility of the different layers of a cathedral's life means that the cathedral will not always be best described in terms of community, or in terms of gathered congregation. The cathedral is the cathedral principally because it is 'the seat of the bishop and a centre for worship and mission'.[6] In what sense is or can the cathedral be the bishop's church, with a responsibility to the diocese as a whole?

The difficulty of determining whether the Sunday congregation is a gathered layer of local community or a representation of the universal Church indicates the problem of drawing sharp boundaries round any definitions of cathedral. But there are some senses in which the cathedral is visibly a diocesan church. The life of the diocese is embodied in such different ways as the names of the prebends on the stalls in the choir, a map of the diocese on the cathedral walls, the regular pattern of intercession for the parishes, the prominence of the bishop's cathedra, and the responsibility the chapter takes for sustaining and supporting the bishop's teaching ministry. There are the distinctive liturgies that occur regularly each year: the ordinations, the service for the admission of Readers, the diocesan festivals for the ministry of healing, the Mothers' Union, the lay pastoral assistants, and particularly the gathering of the clergy and other ministers on Maundy Thursday to reinvigorate their sacrificial commitment at the start of the Triduum. And there are the other occasions, less liturgical but all concerned to build the sense of belonging together in, and responsibility for, the common life of the diocese – a primary visitation, a diocesan festival, a synod, a lecture, a party to bid farewell to a retiring colleague or to welcome a new one. All these promote the unity of the diocese by drawing people from the parishes to engage in a common task together.

The model of Church to the fore on these occasions will frequently – whether there is a liturgy or not – be sacramental. What is being set before people is a sacramental pattern of unity, of a whole which is greater than the sum of the parts, and which transcends the fragmentary layers of community divided not only by geography, but also by class, age and race. By virtue of the Church's relationship to Christ, 'the Church is a kind of sacrament of intimate union with God and of the unity of all humankind; that is, she is a sign and instrument of such union and unity'.[7] Among the bishop's responsibilities are to be a focus of unity, to guard the faith and to promote the Church's mission. The cathedral makes these concerns visible. Its liturgical expression on such occasions will be inclusive and will work with a style that is neither grandly cathedral nor narrowly parochial, but inclusively diocesan. That goes particularly for the music – how badly we need a classless musical style, free of churchmanship connotations, a new Taizé or its equivalent. And which cathedrals have succeeded in teaching the whole diocese something like the Rimsky-Korsakov Lord's Prayer, which can be sung in every church and be a literal embodiment of common prayer? This principle also goes for the style of celebration: what pattern of concelebration, what use of those who are in distinctive deacon's orders, what part properly given to lay people, what signals of inclusion for the handicapped, especially the profoundly deaf, are important to make this an inclusive, not an exclusive, celebration? And while there will be expectations that the bishop himself will properly be the speaker or preacher on many of these occasions, when may he properly delegate, or fulfil his responsibility by inviting a particular preacher, or when is it suitable to team-teach with his episcopal colleagues or with members of the chapter? The task of guarding the faith is one that he is unlikely to be competent to exercise on his own in every area, and his colleagues in the cathedral chapter are going to be among his primary resources. The cathedral will also be the focus for any links the diocese may have with the Church overseas, whether in the Third World, or with the Anglican Communion or with other Churches. The visibility of such links at the praying heart of the diocese is an important sign of where they stand in the cathedral's priorities. It is as important for the cathedral to share the diocese's commitment to mission, and to support and make real the bishop's ministry as the leader of mission in the diocese, as for the diocese to share the cathedral's commitment to the excellence of liturgical worship.

At the other end of the scale, when it comes to the 'occasional offices', can there be any place for a baptism or funeral in the cathedral which does not reflect the sense of 'whole Church' that the cathedral carries? What is the place in the cathedral of a private baptism? Is there no layer of the cathedral as community into which that celebration fits? And conversely, is there any justification for the sacraments of baptism and confirmation being administered other than in the cathedral? The celebration of major liturgies of baptism and confirmation in the cathedral, where candidates are drawn together from all over the diocese, says clearly that confirmation is not a parochial event where some minister in episcopal orders has to be drafted in to legitimise the proceedings, but a rite of association with the bishop which has implications for the development of the whole Church in the diocese. The same is true of rites of ordination. Even if these are celebrated in parish churches from time to time, every effort ought to be made to ensure that the style of celebration, as well as the text, is exactly the same as what happens in the cathedral. Whenever I ordain out of the cathedral, I make a point of taking at least four members of the chapter with me to support my ministry, and use the same set of matching vestments for them and the newly ordained as we use in the cathedral.

As the cathedral reflects, embodies and sustains the bishop's ministry of guarding and teaching the faith, and of providing a visible focus of unity for the diocese, so the cathedral has a responsibility to support and exemplify the bishop's role in celebrating the sacraments and providing leadership to the diocese in worship and in mission.

Concelebration, presidency and liturgical leadership

What does such a model imply for the principal cathedral Eucharist on Sunday? First, the model of unity in diversity needs to be apparent, and is not well served by those cathedrals who continue to use the 'three sacred ministers' of the medieval and Tridentine High Mass, however aesthetically pleasing that may appear visually, while others sit in stalls in choir or assist as ministers of communion. I am no great believer in the modern Roman theories of concelebration as co-consecration, nor a defender of clerical huddles which model the us –them divide. All that is functionally necessary is an assembly of Christian people with the bishop or a priest to preside, and a deacon to assist.[8] But I believe firmly that the chapter, a corporate body with responsibility for the leadership of the cathedral's life and ministry, ought to be visible side by side at the altar. This form of concelebration models shared responsibility under a gracious presidency, and that is how the chapter ought to be seen liturgically. In this context, well-planned 'concelebration' gives the opportunity to include clergy from other parts of the diocese and those with specialist ministries who do not have a parochial base, and to make their inclusion visible. It is an important sign of that collegiality and hospitality which is at the the centre of each cathedral's life and witness, and which relates not just to the cathedral as community, but to the cathedral as the bishop's church. For a parish group or visiting party to see their priest included by the chapter is a powerful sign that the cathedral community is at that moment modelling the life of the diocese – the wider Church – and not simply its own introspective life.

Consideration of concelebration raises the question of

presidency. Who is the appropriate president of the celebration on what occasion? Certainly, anyone who has no structural or pastoral link with the assembly – such as a retired canon, or a visiting parish priest, or a diocesan officer – would be an inappropriate president of the cathedral's principal rite. Authority for presiding derives from the bishop, and is given to parish priests with whom the bishop shares the cure of souls, 'which is both yours and mine', so that they may preside in his stead when he cannot be in that particular parish (which is most of the time!) – although whenever he is present, the bishop is normally the president of the rite. In the cathedral it is important to think out clearly the ecclesiological models, as well as the theological issues involved. In the model of cathedral as Benedictine-style community, it may well be appropriate for the dean to preside, even if the bishop is there. In Salisbury, for example, the bishop is also a canon with a prebendal stall, and from time to time it is appropriate for the bishop to take part in such a celebration as a member of the chapter. In some of the other models of the cathedral – when, for example, there is a diocesan or gathered congregation, or a diocesan-wide celebration at the principal Sunday Eucharist – then it would be appropriate for the bishop to preside. Many Benedictine communities have a custom that the duty monk for the week presides at the weekday celebrations, with the abbot standing immediately behind him, visibly delegating his authority.

Normally, however, simply because the bishop is elsewhere in the diocese, another priest will preside in the cathedral, as in any parish. Should it always be the dean? No, because the dean is the community's leader, not the source of sacramental authority, and the chapter's leadership responsibility should be seen to be exercised collaboratively among those who are competent to do so. What makes no theological or liturgical sense at all is for the presidency to be delegated to priests who are not members of the chapter, especially on the grounds that only such priests may be competent to sing.

And related to presidency is the question of how far the cathedral's principal liturgy should use the same basic texts as the parishes of the diocese. Cathedrals have the opportunity to affirm or lead developments in liturgy. If they do not like what they find, they ought to contribute to its improvement, and persuade the diocese and the wider Church to follow, not merely invent their own. People should be able to look to their cathedral for a liturgical lead, not for uncanonical subversion! Building a memorable store of congregational texts, especially in responsive material, is an important task for sustaining common prayer in the Church. Those responsive parts of the service that are genuinely congregational – the responses to the greeting, to the gospel, and at the dismissal, to name but three – need to have an identity throughout the diocese. The same is true for texts like the Lord's Prayer. Whether said or sung, they are properly the whole assembly's, and the cathedral has a responsibility to use and to teach musical settings of these which any congregation can use: responsive texts, dialogues and acclamations are not opportunities for elaborate choir settings.

THE CATHEDRAL AS HERALD AND PROPHET

Where is the prophetic voice of the Church heard? The answer may be that it is heard in the cathedral's programme of debates, dialogues, sermons, consultations and celebrations – yet people may absorb more, or notice more, or be touched at a deeper level, by some visible image, by what is commissioned in stained glass, statuary, engraving and textiles.

Although it is possible to reduce even large spaces to a sense of chaos by the clutter of causes, nevertheless the Amnesty candle, or the Prisoners of Conscience window, or the visibility of the three oils for healing, making new disciples and consecration, can all be powerful signals and sharp reminders to worshipper and visitor alike. Not every cathedral has the opportunity for a wholesale reordering, but most can attend to the balance between what the cathedral proclaims about the key elements of the Christian faith and the way in which that faith is spelt out today. The main liturgical spaces should rehearse the sacramental signs of our encounter with God. How visible is the font? Is there a large Bible, open for visitors to read the gospel of the day? Is there a significant cross that proclaims the redemption, or just a whole series of decorative crosses that lose the impact? Is the principal altar well-lit and the focus of the building? What stands at the climax of the journey? If key elements like these take people on a journey through the main spaces, may it be possible to reinvigorate the use of the subsidiary chapels, which circle round the main spaces, as focuses for particular and contemporary examples of how the faith we own is lived out? The chapel where the oils are kept (and can they be kept visible, not locked away in a cupboard or aumbry?) is a natural place for prayer for the sick, and may be where the Eucharist is celebrated on those days when the sick are a special focus; or it may be that this is where the congregation moves for the intercessions at the end of Evensong on the day of the week when the sick are prayed for specially. And there will be another chapel, perhaps where the sacrament is reserved, where a unity candle will burn on Thursdays, and where intercession at midday or at the end of Thursday Evensong will be focused.

But other chapels can gather particular and more specific focuses. There is a growing awareness, for example, of the widespread nature of child abuse; and many cathedrals have a particular charitable concern because of a local voluntary organisation or the commitment of a member of the chapter. For example, Coventry has an annual service for road accident victims; Norwich has a chapel which is the focus of prayer for innocent victims, and for religious dialogue; the Prisoners of

Conscience window in Salisbury articulates a major concern for justice and human rights, and is not mere decorative wallpaper.

These focuses, and many others, spring from the cathedral's engagement with local concerns, particular charities, and the interests of the members of the chapter and the diocese as a whole at any one time. The special services which take place annually and which are focused on these concerns are a significant part of the cathedral's prophetic ministry. What is it that people want to celebrate? What hopes and fears, concerns and longings, do they bring? How can the cathedral help them to find a language in which to express their anger as well as their hope, their trust as well as their commitment, as they set their story against the story of what God has done for us in Christ? They need a welcome, they want to be recognised, they look for God's blessing. But they also need to be challenged by the Gospel, so that their work is shaped by that encounter, and they are brought to a moment of transformation. Without that element, any liturgy is defective.

It is no easy task to craft a liturgy that will offer a transforming experience for a congregation who have assembled for a particular occasion, drawn together by a common cause rather than by conscious ecclesial allegiance. Sometimes it will involve a simple movement of the congregation to stand by a memorial or around a symbol; sometimes it will be through an evocative sound – the Last Post or a piper's lament; sometimes through a simple action – dipping a sprig of rosemary into holy water, and casting it into the grave. Liturgical archaeologists may not be the best judges of what is needed, or of what will touch a deep memory or strike a chord. The challenge of the prophetic word demands a ritual vehicle for response, and we fail our congregations if we do not also give them an opportunity to respond in their language, to make a gesture not only of identification, but of self-giving.

Cathedrals are well used to taking up these opportunities.

There may be a judges' service, services for teachers, governors and students on Education Sunday or at the start of the academic year. The Children's Society will want a Christingle service, and Christian Aid week is well established. But what other areas of concern does the cathedral believe should be championed? What pattern of seminar, discussion, worship, party, follow-up and visible focus in the cathedral will give these important out-workings of the faith a real presence in the cathedral's liturgical life? Cathedrals have an opportunity and a duty to think and speak prophetically, and their independence from direct accountability to their congregation or to the bishop is an important safeguard in exercising a truly prophetic ministry. Cathedrals can, and should, afford to be unpopular in speaking those truths to the Church, as well as to the wider community, which they may not want to hear.

There are two theological emphases behind this mode of being cathedral. First, there is the desire to stand with people in their pain and frustration. If we cannot enter imaginatively into this, our liturgies will always be bland and soothing; we shall appear disinterested, if not patronising. To stand in solidarity with the unloved at the foot of the cross has to be a genuine part of our prayer, and cathedrals as institutions do not naturally find themselves standing there. And second, there is the apostolic charge to preach the Gospel, to preach change, to bring hope. Here again, the incarnational strand of solidarity is necessarily complemented by a redemptive call to change the world. We cannot abandon or soft-pedal one of these strands without betraying our commission to embody the whole Christ, in both his incarnation and redemption, whether we are talking of our encounter with specific organisations or expressed needs on the one hand, or about the individuals who come through the cathedral's doors day by day on the other.

Some fundamental questions emerge from this analysis which are beyond the scope of this chapter, but with which cathedrals wishing to move beyond a reactive mode in their theological thinking and liturgical planning need to engage. How do cathedrals make a conscious choice about which model or models of Church to use, and with whom do they consult as they make their choice? Do the models they choose have theological coherence with one another? How do they relate to the life of the whole Church? And within this process other questions emerge. Whose cathedral is it? What are its principal tasks? With whom are those tasks worked out and how are they planned, owned and prepared? These are important questions for those cathedrals which are concerned to move their liturgy beyond a fairly unreflective rehearsal of the English cathedral tradition and its largely institutional base.

I began this chapter with the claim that 'cathedrals are true because they make and celebrate liturgy'. The Church's task in worship is to make the transforming nature of our relationship with God accessible. Cathedrals have an unrivalled opportunity to proclaim and interpret this in their worship. So if it is in liturgy that our belief about the nature of the Church is made visible, then we will be helped by recognising a plurality of theological models of the Church. Each of these will articulate a way of being Church appropriate to a particular group or layer within the community's life, and each will be expressed in different liturgical patterns – patterns which together will be facets of a theologically coherent whole.

FIVE

MUSIC IN THESE STONES

RICHARD SHEPHARD

It cannot be denied that the most important function of a cathedral is its offering of daily worship. Other activities – mission, evangelism, teaching, preaching and even the provision of a seat for the bishop – are bound to be of secondary importance if we believe that 'the chief end of man is to glorify God and to worship him for ever'. Worship comes in many forms: even in cathedrals there is a great variety of said and sung services and devotions, and it needs to be recognised that a said service is as valid an act of worship as a service containing music. But one of the glories of the English cathedrals is the tradition of sung services, in particular Evensong, which has come to be perceived almost as a self-sufficient art form. It is, in its dignified words and appropriate music, a thing of great artistic beauty – but it is not an end in itself. The tradition of such choral offices serves to assist the members of the body of Christ in their worship of almighty God. What that tradition is, however, is sometimes less than obvious.

The interest in cathedral choirs, the spate of recordings, the multitude of tours, all testify to there being something special about what has come to be called the 'cathedral tradition'. How splendid it would be if it were true, as Canon C. C. Bell stated,[1] that at York, James the deacon was appointed in

627 to found a song school for the instruction of choristers. True, Bede does state that James began to teach people to sing the music of the Church according to the Uses of Rome.[2] However, to infer from a passing reference that a choral foundation as we now know it was extant in 627 is romantic wishful thinking.

Equally misguided is the idea that somehow there has been a natural progression over the last 1000 years, through the changes of the Reformation, to the situation which obtains today: a kind of Darwinian evolutionary process. There is a wealth of evidence which suggests that, far from being a *cathedral* tradition, the corpus of church music and the habit of performing it to a high standard comes from a royal background. Byrd, Tallis, Gibbons, Purcell, Blow, Greene, Boyce, were all London-based and had an important connection with the Chapel Royal. Boyce's collection, *Cathedral Music*, was an important landmark in the wider dissemination of choral music, but, in general terms, the tradition was firmly London-based. The contrast between the capital and the provinces is clearly pointed out by the first great provincial contributor to the tradition, S. S. Wesley:

> Painful and dangerous is the position of a young musician who, after acquiring great knowledge of his art in the Metropolis, joins a country Cathedral. At first he can scarcely believe that the mass of error and inferiority in which he has to participate is habitual and irremediable. He thinks he will reform matters, gently, and without giving offence; but he soon discovers that it is his approbation and not his advice that is needed. The Choir is 'the best in England' (such being the belief at most cathedrals) and, if he give trouble in his attempts at improvement, he would be, by some Chapters, at once voted a person with whom they 'cannot get on smoothly'.[3]

Wesley was writing in 1849, at a time when it is quite clear that the standard of choral worship was at best mediocre and at worst execrable. We have to accept that chapter act-books will tend to chronicle the unusual rather than the mundane, nevertheless during the nineteenth century there do seem to have been numerous problems connected with cathedral choirs. At Lichfield, for example, in 1854, two of the singing men were over the age of 80. From many chapter act-books come complaints about the incompetence of singers, on the occasions when they actually attended service, absenteeism being another frequent cause for complaint. The most famous case of absenteeism was at Hereford on Easter Day 1833, when, for the first performance of S. S. Wesley's anthem, 'Blessed be the God and Father', only one singing man was present, the dean's butler.

Wesley's *A Few Words on Cathedral Music*, repays study. Wesley, by all accounts a difficult man, describes forcibly the situation in provincial cathedrals. While there have been great improvements in the standard of performance, many of his criticisms still hold true. He argues that the standards expected of professional musicians in the secular world should be expected of church musicians. He criticises poor standards of composition:

> Thus it is that the Choral Service of the Church presents not one feature in its present mode of performance which can interest or affect the well-informed auditor; except so far as it may remind him of a grandeur that exists no longer.[4]

He sees clearly that poor standards in performance can be glossed over:

> The illusive and fascinating effect of musical sound in a Cathedral unfortunately serves to blunt criticism, and cast a veil over defects otherwise unbearable. No coat of varnish can do for a picture what the exquisitely reverber-

ating qualities of a Cathedral do for music. And then, the Organ! What a multitude of sins does *that* cover![5]

He also, quite rightly, criticises the clergy for failing to give music proper importance in the liturgy:

> The prospect of bringing the Clergy to a just sense of the claims of music in the Cathedral Service of this country seems all but hopelessly remote. They still, in the main, view their own labours as all-important, and disparage the art in its most important bearings. The arts, in their connection with religion, are systematically decried, and *preaching* but too often viewed as the one thing needful in the public services.[6]

Wesley's importance lies in his being the first great *cathedral* musician to compose for cathedrals. His compositions are of variable quality, but the best of them force one to wonder what he might have achieved had he been free of the baleful influence of the organ loft. Interestingly the three composers who were Wesley's juniors, and who are generally credited with a large part in the renaissance of English music in general and cathedral music in particular, were none of them cathedral musicians: Hubert Parry (1848–1918), Charles Villiers Stanford (1852–1924) and Charles Wood (1866–1926). All three men held Oxbridge academic posts, and Parry and Stanford also taught in music colleges. Their works form the staple diet of most cathedrals, and by and large it is a wholesome diet.

But where in all this is the 'cathedral tradition', and wherein lay the impulse for the development of the cathedral musical repertoire? The impetus to improve standards came not from Archbishops' Commissions or even from the excellent work of the Royal School of Church Music. The impetus undoubtedly came from broadcasting and recordings, and pre-eminent among the recorded choirs must be that of King's College, Cambridge. Successive musical directors, from Boris Ord onwards, ensured that church music reached a far wider audience. It began to have an existence outside a liturgical framework – as a result of which, expectations were raised. People expected to hear church music *inside* the liturgy sung to as high a standard as that on the records to which they could listen at home. In many cases they must have been bitterly disappointed, but gradually Oxbridge choral scholars began to replace the old freehold lay clerks, and standards rose. Not until well into this century did many cathedral choirs achieve standards which would have been approaching the acceptable in the secular world of music making.

At the time when cathedral choirs were fighting their way towards a largely uniform standard, the forces of liturgical reform were working towards the Alternative Service Book (ASB). In itself, liturgical revision has had little effect on cathedral worship: a more regular Eucharist (frequently Rite A) has replaced Matins in many cathedrals, but Evensong has so far remained untouched. But the ASB, and the Archbishops' Commissions on Church Music and on Cathedrals, have raised questions about the role of cathedrals and inevitably about the place of music within the life of the cathedral. For whom is the worship intended? Who should perform it? What should be performed? These are three fundamental questions which continue to be asked; and it is right that cathedrals should consider these questions carefully if they are to avoid the frequently levelled charge of complacency.

FOR WHOM IS THE WORSHIP INTENDED?

The answer to the first question – for whom is the worship intended? – is generally answered by the single word, God. True, all worship is directed towards God – but cathedrals provide the opportunity for many to participate in acts of worship of a high artistic standard and of a musical and aesthetic quality inevitably lacking in much simpler parochial offerings. The nature of participation is, however, frequently misunderstood – for, in a cathedral service, every worshipper need not be busy. In fact, one of the joys of cathedral worship is that non-performers can be carried along without any exertion on their part. Numbers of people attending Evensong are bound to vary from cathedral to cathedral, but there has been a substantial increase nationally over the last few decades.

While it is right that cathedral authorities should acknowledge the existence of a cathedral congregation, it is important that its role and influence should be understood. Cathedral worship is an alternative to parish worship; it is not parish worship writ large. The mission of a cathedral is to a wider constituency than that of a parish, so the role and importance of the congregation must be less than in a parish. In matters of liturgy and music the wishes and preferences of a self-selecting congregation may well not be representative of the expectations of the rest of the diocese or the wider Church. Cathedral congregations, then, need to be treated with caution.

WHO SHOULD PERFORM THE MUSIC?

The musical standard in cathedrals is very varied, but then so are the cathedrals themselves. There is a tendency to assume that all cathedrals should provide the same sort of musical diet – sung daily offices, and sung Eucharist on a Sunday – with the addition of local eccentricities. But is this really wise? Of course, the sung services of the cathedrals need to be not only preserved but also improved – but cathedral X in the middle of a northern industrial town is doing a very different job from cathedral Y in a small southern market town. There are the similarities – the great diocesan occasions, the carol services, the services of national importance – but cathedral X may well have an importance in the industrial life of the diocese or in caring for the homeless, while cathedral Y's mission, apart from being to the comfortably-off middle classes, may well have an international dimension. Cathedral Z, by contrast, may be too small to host huge events, so other venues must be found.

Given this wide diversity of foundation, it is difficult to make critical judgements on cathedral music as a whole at the end of the twentieth century. When approaching the matter, however, it is important to be guided by the principle that critical judgement should not be suspended merely because the music happens to be taking place as part of the liturgy. It is true that there are some excellent choirs and choirmasters, but the general standard is certainly not as high as some would assert. In many cases, the problems associated with cathedral choirs have led to performances which are frequently poor – although often disguised by Wesley's acoustical varnish.

These problems are not new. To deal with the front rows first. Although there has been a decline in the number of applicants for choristerships during the second half of the century, information tends to suggest that the quality of applicants is higher than it once was.[7] Before the last war, choristerships were seen by parents from the lower socio-economic groups as a way of getting a reasonable and cheap education for their sons in return for their singing. Broadly speaking they were right – although the quality of education was frequently not of the highest. In recent years, however, with the marked improvement in the educational standards of choir schools,[8] choristers have been coming from the professional classes and, despite the efforts of the Choir Schools' Association, it has been difficult to widen the socio-economic catchment area in those cathedrals which have choir schools. The cathedrals without schools have to recruit without the incentive of educational scholarships, but they find it easier to recruit across the social spectrum. Both systems give the singing boys and girls great opportunities, and one of the most welcome developments in recent years is the way in which cathedral clergy, head teachers and organists have been prepared to share problems and to learn from each other.

The addition of girls to the musical strength of many cathedrals has presented foundations with some financial and administrative problems, but there are many benefits: for the first time girls are allowed to participate actively in cathedral worship; they are being given the same educational and musical opportunities as boys. In addition to the benefits to the girls themselves, their inclusion should enable cathedrals to provide a wider and more varied programme of musical activities, both in the cathedral and also in the diocese.

Moving back a row to the lay clerks, we find that throughout the history of cathedral choirs there have been arguments between singing men and organists and deans and chapters. Frequently these arguments have been about money or drink or debauchery of varying kinds – perhaps the most interesting case being that of John Farrant who attempted to kill the dean of Salisbury.[9] Wesley struck a new note when he suggested that lay singers should be as well rehearsed as musicians in the secular world.[10] He also noted the problem of a man who has two types of employment: 'rendering him, but too often, a tradesman amongst singers, and a singer amongst tradesmen'.

One way of ensuring that a lay clerk managed to earn a living wage was to employ him to teach in the choir school. This cosy system is less easy to operate nowadays when head teachers must look for the best educationalists, and are unwilling to be used as a source of income in order to keep the choir going. Money, however, is not the answer to the problem. If cathedrals suddenly paid lay clerks a living wage for singing a couple of hours a day, what implications would this have on other cathedral employees? Even if this hurdle could be jumped by using the supply-and-demand argument, the likely result of a large salary increase would be to ensure that second-rate and third-rate singers had a comfortable and secure job for life. Where then would be the striving for excellence in worship?

Nobody becomes a lay clerk for the sake of the financial rewards – their rewards are musical, spiritual, cultural. If we accept that, for the unsocial hours they work, lay clerks are not overpaid financially, then it is important that the intangible rewards of the job must be there in full measure. The obverse of this is that there must be a regular and realistic assessment of the vocal abilities of lay clerks. Understandably, chapters are unwilling to dismiss a faithful servant of the cathedral because his voice is not what it once was – but the failure to do this strikes at the heart of the attempt to offer the best in worship to God.

The person charged to be a musical chief executive is the organist, or master of the choir, or director of music, or whatever. The proliferation of titles gives a hint of the problems connected with this role. Until well into this century it was the custom for the organists to play the organ and for the choir to look after itself. Choir practices were frequently a formality because in many cathedrals, the repertoire, though large, did not change. It sounds a strange system, but on one level it worked. The organist's expertise was as a keyboard executant: the lay clerks were professional singers who may have had inadequate voices, but who, by and large, sang accurately. The services happened without too many disasters; the congregations were small, and duty had been done.

The modern system is very different. Organists no longer do what they were trained to do – play the organ: they conduct the choir, leaving the assistant to preside at the keys. This is an oversimplification, but there seems to have been little recognition of the fact that the job has changed. In the 1950s and 1960s, the organist and his assistant would rarely appear in the cathedral on the same day. At Gloucester, for example, the organist Herbert Sumsion would play on Mondays, Tuesdays, Wednesdays and Sundays, and the assistant John Sanders would conduct the unaccompanied service on Fridays and would play on Saturdays. Occasionally the organist would conduct an unaccompanied Eucharist setting, but his appearance as a conductor was rare. Nowadays organists appear at virtually every service and conduct everything possible, including psalms, hymns and amens.

Both the Archbishops' Commission on Church Music,[11] and the Archbishops' Commission on Cathedrals,[12] give clear notice that this change in role needs to be acknowledged and legislated for. If the main task of an organist is to be a choral director, administrator and adviser to the dean and chapter on all matters musical, then it is unwise to insist that all applicants must be organists. Some degree of keyboard facility is undoubtedly needed in order to take a choir practice, but the skills and knowledge required to be a choral director are not those acquired by study of the organ repertoire. Knowledge of the choral repertoire is far more important, and a formulation of a policy which states clearly the rationale behind choice of music is something which many cathedrals need. The carbon-copy music scheme, which repeats music on a termly or yearly basis, will not do. Within the framework of the liturgical year there is endless scope for variety and experiment.

WHAT MUSIC SHOULD BE PERFORMED?

This variety and experiment need to be woven into the fabric of cathedral musical activity. There are opportunities both in the cathedral and also in the wider community of city, county and diocese. In the cathedral, there needs to be a clearer idea of what the liturgical music is for, and what it is not for. It is not a means of rehearsing for a forthcoming recording or tour. It is not an indulgence of the organists, lay clerks or clergy in their own personal whims and preferences. It is there to assist the people of God in their worship.

Within the tradition (even if the exact nature of the tradition is slightly opaque) there is a wealth of fine music. The great composers such as Byrd, Tallis and Purcell should figure largely on all music lists. But on the lower slopes of Parnassus there are many composers whose best efforts deserve to be sung regularly. There can sometimes be a snobbery, particularly about music from the eighteenth and nineteenth centuries, but many pieces from this era deserve regular performances. The assumption that all Tudor music is good is as laughable as the assumption that all twentieth-century music is good.

When it comes to contemporary music, there are problems. Jonathan Harvey pleads very strongly for a closer relationship between Church and composers: 'There has been an almost total failure of communication between the Church and the liveliest composers of our day, a gap filled by "local" composers, the men on the spot, organists, etc.'[13]

Leaving aside the rather obvious comment that the greatest of all church composers, J. S. Bach, could be dismissed as 'a "local" composer, the man on the spot, organist, etc.', Professor Harvey does identify a real problem. There has indeed been a failure of communication, but that failure has been to some extent the fault of the composers. If music is in essence a form of communication, it seems less than adequate to write in a way that fails to communicate with the worshippers for whom it was written. It cannot be denied that much twentieth-century music is inaccessible to many people; the fault is not theirs, neither should they feel guilty for it. For surely, in divine worship more than anywhere else, it is essential that the composer should control his desire to express his inmost *angst* and *weltschmerz* and should instead concentrate on providing music which, at the lowest level, does not irritate the worshippers. William Mathias expresses succinctly where the duties of the church composer lie:

> Church music composed now must have something new to say which marks it out in one way or another (and

84

there is never only one way) as belonging to our time. Second: it must nevertheless be such that it does not radically interfere with, or cut across, the act of Worship of which it forms an essential part. Third: it should be the best of which a composer is capable in the sense that one may not permit artistic triviality in the Service of God.[14]

This is not to say that cathedrals should abdicate their responsibility of commissioning new works to adorn the liturgy. There is good reason for pride in the number of services and anthems which have been paid for by cathedrals in the last few decades. What composers need to recognise, however, is that they are writing for the moment. It is impossible to write with an eye cocked towards eternity; the composer must, as Mathias advocates, do his very best and then leave the future life of his brainchild to posterity. Some must, like Salieri, survive to see themselves become extinct.[15]

The choice of music, then, needs to take into consideration a whole host of criteria with regard to achieving a reasonable cross-section of the best English music from a wide variety of styles and dates. In addition to this there is the wealth of music from Europe. It is excellent to be able to hear Mozart sung liturgically, and to be able to enjoy some of the Schutz psalm settings – but, at the risk of being insular, we should not allow the best of English compositions to be driven out by inferior foreign imports. As with Tudor music, not all French or Belgian music is good. Here again, the clergy and laity responsible for choice must see the wider picture, and perhaps forego their yearning for more of the *petits maîtres* from across the Channel. It is perhaps salutary to remember the dean who stated forcibly, 'I am not going to spend hours wandering around in Wesley's *Wilderness*' – and refused to allow that masterpiece to be performed in his cathedral. Wesley's *Wilderness* remains, but where is the dean? In similar vein, a lecturer justly castigated Dean Foxley-Norris for forbidding a performance of *The Dream of Gerontius* in York Minster, and for applying the veto to a Byron memorial in Westminster Abbey.[16] Titcombe pointed out the pleasure gained in contemplating Elgar and Byron strolling through the Elysian Fields, perhaps catching sight of Foxley-Norris on celestial latrine duty.

The daily offices are the lifeblood of cathedral music, but there is so much more that could be done. To perform a monthly Bach cantata in place of a sermon could be an artistic and spiritual experience for the hearers (epithets which can seldom be applied to sermons). Concerts of readings and music for Holy Week, greater use of the architectural space of the buildings, collaboration with other organisations such as universities and colleges – all will enhance the tradition. Many of these things are being done throughout the country, but it is all too easy to use the daily services as an excuse for lack of vision. They are crucially important, but there is life beyond.

There is frequently a call for cathedral musicians to include music of a more popular and simple style in the repertoire. Choruses, worship songs and Taizé music do not figure largely in cathedral worship. Here we step into the minefield of subjective judgement: what is good, what is appropriate, what is worthy? There is no doubt that, for some people, choruses with repetitive texts and music are of enormous help in their personal devotions. For others, the simplicity of a Taizé chant or a worship song performs a valuable function. Given that these forms of music are widely used in the Church, it seems wrong to exclude them from cathedrals. It would, however, be unwise to attempt to mix them into the formality of choral Evensong. There are, however, other opportunities: an occasional praise service in the nave; a more intimate late-night service in a side chapel; with imagination much more could be done, provided that cathedral clergy and musicians abandon defensive positions.

The attitude of some cathedral musicians to the rest of the diocese has been rather like that of Rat to the Wide World, to paraphrase Kenneth Grahame:[17] 'Beyond the cathedral comes the Wide Diocese, and that's something that doesn't matter, either to you or me. I've never been there, and I'm never going.'

The problem is that what goes on musically in the parishes differs markedly from what goes on in the cathedral. This does not matter in the slightest, nor is any one form of worship more valid than another. So what could cathedral musicians do at a diocesan level? Visits by the cathedral choir to sing around the diocese have certainly given great pleasure in many counties. As a one-off event, the cathedral choir singing for a parish service or giving a recital is undoubtedly a good thing – but there is a need for greater collaboration over church music in dioceses. This is not to say that all parish music should aspire to be like cathedral music. That was tried in the nineteenth century, when the local, traditional gallery bands were replaced by robed choirs and organs. Neither should well-meaning but woolly canons attempt to turn great cathedrals into parish churches writ large. The mission of the cathedral is (or should be) much wider than to the group of self-selecting regular worshippers. Instead, the musical staff of cathedrals should be used more as a teaching resource for the diocese.

Much good can be done by a cathedral musician teaching a parish congregation some new hymns or choruses, or perhaps breaking down the fear of Anglican chant or even plainsong. There are some fine musicians among cathedral lay clerks, clergy and organists who could do excellent work on an occasional basis in the wider diocese. There is always a place for a large diocesan event – but the greater need is for something less grand, less threatening, more homely. There is a real need in parishes for musicians to visit, to take congregational or choir rehearsals, to instruct or advise on the music available for parishes with limited resources. A visit from a member of the cathedral music staff is of enormous benefit, both practically and psychologically. There has already been much good work done in various dioceses – but there is a temptation for cathedral staff to regard themselves as guardians of a sacred musical treasure, which they are willing to display to others in the cathedral setting, but which they feel will not travel well.

As the General Synod contemplates sweeping changes to cathedral administration, in the wake of the Howe Report,[18] at a time when people in all walks of life are being called upon to justify their activity and when old certainties are being questioned, it is inevitable that expenditure on cathedral music should come under the spotlight. For too long, cathedral musicians have dealt with any questioning of the expense of sung worship by a superior reference to the gospel story of the precious ointment.[19] To an extent they are right. Cathedral music is a precious luxury which will appeal to fewer people than many other forms of music, but there is no doubt that attendances at cathedral services are growing, and that, as previously mentioned, the dissemination of church music on CD and radio has had a great effect on the public. The phenomenal success of recent plainsong recordings could be a mere aberration, but it could signal a search on the part of the listening public for something beyond the world of the concert hall. If this is indeed the case, and it may well be so, then cathedral musicians are well-placed to cater for this need.

There is every reason why the music of our cathedrals should draw people in. There is nothing wrong in attending services for the music rather than for the religion: who knows where one ends and the other starts? This is an enfolding activity in which the cathedral and its music act as a magnet. By contrast, the cathedral should be outward looking, seeing itself as a resource for the rest of the diocese; indeed, if cathedral musicians prove themselves to be indispensable in the diocese, then criticism and resentment of the financial and human resources needed by cathedral music can be answered.

SIX

BUILDING AND CHERISHING

Cathedrals as buildings

ANDREW ANDERSON

The cathedrals of England are found, implanted like pace-makers, in the hearts of cities and towns – visible in some cases for miles, the focal point of market-places and civic squares. In spite of the high-rise buildings which have transformed the urban skyline in recent years, most cathedrals remain domi-nant townscape features. They rise from the ruins of old abbeys, nestle in the corners of closes and college quadrangles, or rest, like intricate caskets, on carpets of mown grass. At Ely, the cathedral seems the sole reason for the city's existence. Some have a homely, almost feminine, character: others are more daunting – intellectual exercises calling for an effort of the brain as well as a response of the heart. They may touch an emotional nerve or, as the dean of St Paul's wrote in *The Times* in 1992, 'give man a glimpse of eternity'.[1] For many, they confirm their European identity. A more down-to-earth explanation of the fascination they hold for the thousands of tourists and pilgrims who flock through their doors is the maze-like complexity of their ground-floor plans, the mys-terious roped-off sanctuaries and stalls, the curtained thrones, the inaccessible subterranean vaults and crypts, the dim side chapels, the seen but forbidden high-level galleries and passageways, tempting the adventurous but closed to public access by safety-conscious administrators and local authority building inspectors. Cathedrals just ask to be explored. They invite curiosity – which is probably why, in the ones which charge for admission, only the disadvantaged seem put off.

A cathedral may be the seat of the bishop and a centre of worship and mission, but it is much *more* than that, as shown by the outpouring of popular sympathy and support which followed the York Minster fire in July 1984, and as evidenced by the widespread public protest in the 1980s at the sale of treasures and the removal of old glass. A whole constituency of people feel they have a stake in cathedrals and, moreover, use them for their own ends: from aids to meditation and candlelit prayer, to places to warm up on a cold day, or as short cuts when shopping. Candles are an interesting recent phenomenon – clusters of liquid light on metal frames, coating the stone floors with wax or flaming in sand trays. 'Candles make a place come alive', a verger at St Albans told me recently. 'You can see life when you can see candles: it's prayers.' They are also a source of much-needed income.

The statistics are interesting. Of the 42 English Anglican cathedrals, 12 are medieval monastic foundations, 9 are non-monastic medieval institutions, 6 are post-Reformation upgrades and 11 are enlarged parish churches – including St Albans and St Edmundsbury where the nave of the ruined abbey church lies to the east. Four were purpose-built in the last hundred years: Truro (1880–1910) which absorbed the old church of St Mary's; Guildford (1936–61); Liverpool (1904–78) and Coventry (1956–62). All are well documented in books and guides catering for all ages and tastes: outstanding examples include David Edwards' *The Cathedrals of Britain* and Christopher Wilson's *The Gothic Cathedral*,[2] and there are many others.

A church does not have to be large to be a cathedral, and their sizes differ enormously. Two of the oldest foundations

(Carlisle and Oxford) are also among the smallest – smaller than Beverley Minster and Tewkesbury Abbey – and the size of most of the parish church cathedrals has had to be increased. Liverpool has the highest cathedral tower in England; St Albans has the longest nave; Winchester is the longest overall (the longest in Europe); and Salisbury's spire is higher than the dome of St Paul's. Rather than being a story of slow decline, English cathedral building has been more like a volcano in continuous eruption from the tenth century onwards, with a spectacular explosion – St Paul's – between 1675 and 1710, and further steady lava flows in the last 100 years, the last (Liverpool) being the biggest of all. Nor is the era of cathedral building finished: apart from the nave and west front at Portsmouth (completed in 1991) and a planned central tower at St Edmundsbury, St Albans, Chelmsford and Southwark boast major post-war additions, Hereford has a new library, and visitors' centres in the precincts are planned at Canterbury, Norwich and Leicester.

How have these enormous, but basically fragile, buildings survived, in some cases for nearly 1000 years? A practical rather than an inspirational answer is unquestionably the simplicity of their construction, without which, because of their sheer size, maintenance would have been impossible over such a long period of time. One of the most remarkable features of cathedrals is the small number of materials which were used to build them, and are still used to keep them standing: a mere handful – stone, wood, lead, glass, iron, occasionally brick and tiles – and crucially, the absence of external surfaces needing paint and polyvinylchoride sealants which deteriorate and leak. Their other outstanding attribute, not shared by most large modern buildings, is the ease with which all the high-level walls and roofs can be reached for inspection, cleaning and repair, through a network of staircases, walkways and galleries – priceless features which help just as much as the sparse methods of construction to ensure their continuing existence.

For an architect or member of the maintenance staff, an access turret in an aisle or transept is worth a thousand prayers.

You cannot understand cathedrals on their own. They are not isolated works of religious and architectural genius in an otherwise secular landscape. You approach them through a network of smaller churches – over 20,000 or thereabouts nationwide, if you include the unlisted and unused ones and recognisable ruins – flotillas of small vessels clustered round the flagship, miniature versions of the mother ship, held together by a chain of command resembling the Royal Navy's. The commerce between the admiral's headquarters and his fleet has always been lively and two-way. Now, as well as then, the skills of the cathedral workshops spill over into the surrounding countryside, maintaining a distinguished English tradition. In 1484–5 the cellarer of the priory at Norwich 'spent a sum of £24 on the new chancel of Worstead Church', a building which is still in the care of the dean and chapter, and Robert Everard, the master mason who erected Norwich's beautiful nave vault and spire between 1463 and 1472, worked on several churches belonging to the priory. John de Ramsay was almost certainly the mason who built the chapel of Norwich School and Cley Church on the north Norfolk coast, while James Woderofe was probably the designer of the mid fifteenth-century west tower of Wymondham Abbey. The Norwich Cathedral workshops not only helped churches: not content with designing the gates of the 'Prechyngyerd', John Doraunt supplied timbers for the repair of the Peacock Inn in Market Square.[3] Today, at least 15 cathedrals have works departments, some undertaking outside contracting, and the glazing workshops at Canterbury and York operate over radiuses of well over 200 miles.

For all the intensive work which goes into the study of the fabric and into their day-to-day usefulness and maintenance, cathedrals are mysterious shapes, long thin tubes of stone and glass sandwiched between tall, noisy bell towers and slender spires through which pigeons flutter and winds moan, capped by coloured flags and shining weathervanes. If we were not so used to them their sight – the west front of Peterborough, for example – would be extraordinary. While the narrowness of medieval naves and transepts is probably due to the limitations placed by Norman and early thirteenth-century engineering on the span of roof trusses and vaults, and a Gothic nave may owe its length to the need for spectacular processions, Christopher Wilson suggests that the interior was divided up primarily to emphasise the restricted view human beings have, on earth, of the heavenly city which the Gothic cathedral portrayed.[4] Although we no longer believe in celestial cities in the same sense as the builders of Salisbury and Canterbury did, I have felt for a long time that the fascination which draws visitors by their thousands is partly due to the fact that, in wandering round cathedrals, we are wandering round our-selves: peeping into, revisiting and digesting the separate, often disparate pieces of our own lives as we experience them daily in the confused, hurly-burly world outside. We often forget that, in their early days, they were seen alongside, and as complementary to, the castle of the military garrison (at Norwich, Lincoln and Durham, for example): twin, sobering symbols of temporal power. Today the body language of cathedrals is gentler, less threatening. The distant view of St Albans from the M25, the view of Lincoln from the congested streets at the bottom of the hill, the sight of Ely and Durham from the train, gives the Church of England a quieter, more reassuring, less stressful image than it had in the past and is accorded in the press and on radio and TV. Year in, year out, sunlit by day and floodlit by night, cathedrals are there for all to see, regardless of the prevailing meteorological and political conditions or the intensity of the media spotlight.

While cathedrals offer everyone who sees them a glimpse of eternity, you cannot in fact find anything more earthbound if you have, say, to relead the roofs or rehang the bells. With them we come down to earth with a bump – to a world of stresses and strains, forces and counterforces, the chemistry of stone and lead, the action of rain and ice, the pressures exerted by wind and soil movements, all on a scale demanding engineering of the greatest daring when these structures were first conceived. While there is no mystery about how the cathedrals were built, it remains a wonder how these prodigious feats were achieved before the days of steel scaffolding and tower cranes, with only poles lashed together with rope and reed-covered walkways. Another source of astonishment is the innovative imagination of the masons, matching the artistry of the carvers, tilers and glaziers: stone stressed up to (and occasionally beyond) its limits. Although there was nothing in England to match the spectacular collapses at Beauvais (where at one stage only a condemned criminal could be found to go aloft to make the building safe),[5] there were major failures at St Albans, Chichester, Norwich, Ely and elsewhere. Paradoxically, these collapses have led to some of the best, most characteristic English medieval architecture – Robert Wodehurst's beautiful presbytery vault at Norwich and William Hurley's equally impressive mid fourteenth-century star vault at Ely – and we would not have Coventry without the Blitz. While the neo-Gothic cathedrals at Truro, Guildford and Liverpool may be miracles in the sense that today, only a few decades later, expenditure on such a scale is unthinkable, they are unremarkable in engineering terms: it is the Crystal Palace, the railway halls of London and York, and the airship hangars at Cardington which are, from a structural point of view, the cathedrals of the last 100 years.

Apart from commenting on their size, a lot of people seem to think that cathedrals have a distinctive look about them. I sit on two Diocesan Advisory Committees and, at a meeting of one of them recently, we had an application from a church which wanted to install a sink unit at the back of the north aisle. There was no drawing of the unit, but the form stated that it had 'doors of a cathedral style', as if that settled the matter: what more was there to be said? But what does a sink unit with cathedral-style doors look like? I think everyone round the table pictured Gothic-shaped doors – although the Gothic style is by no means confined to cathedrals and not all cathedrals are Gothic – but a deeper message was clearly intended. We were reading comfortable, reassuring words implying: 'Don't worry; the doors may only be oak-faced blockboard but it will be *excellent* oak-faced blockboard, much better than the chipboard you will find anywhere else in the country and therefore worthy of being added to the timeless inventory of a historic Suffolk church'. But do cathedrals have a style of their own, distinct from the buildings which surround them – and if so, how do you describe it? If the word 'cathedral' conjures up the idea of excellence in people's minds, perhaps it is because that is what they are: centres of excellence on all fronts, something broader, more wide-ranging, more secular than centres of worship and mission – excellence in the intellectual and spiritual calibre of the people who run them, excellence in the music and liturgy, excellence in the fittings and works of art which adorn them (John Piper's tapestry at Chichester is an example), excellence in the educational facilities for tourists and young people, excellence in the care of the priceless fabric and the equally priceless contents, excellence in the quality of the granary bread and low-fat meals on offer at refectory counters – places where nothing but the best is expected, and found. Could it be that cathedrals are offering a mentally and physically healthy *lifestyle* which can be transported into our homes and workplaces just as, in the Middle Ages, the monastic communities which inhabited these buildings offered a vision of a life of prayer and study to their turbulent, often violent world?

It is easy – but not in the end very instructive – to get carried away by cathedrals with talk of eternal verities, of angels, ghosts and green men. The importance of these places

stems from their overwhelming physicality – from their function in resisting large structural forces, in standing up to gales
and keeping out prodigious quantities of snow and rain, in
seating substantial numbers of people in reasonable comfort
whatever the conditions outside – something which cannot be
said of football stadiums, which are often the only other local
auditoriums capable of seating a crowd. They are places which
can be accurately measured (to fractions of a centimetre when
movement or stone decay need to be recorded), spaces filled
with electrical wiring and serviced by mechanical hoists and
winches which have to be checked for safety, walls honey-
combed with passageways calling for guard rails. A feeling of
spiritual warmth at choral Evensong needs a boiler (more likely
two or three) in a boiler-house, and the music is dependent as
much on the shape and voicing of the organ pipes (and the
physiology of the vocal chords of the choristers) as on the
imagination of the composer. A cathedral may be priceless, but
each one has to be insured – in most cases for between £30
million and £40 million – figures that do not reflect the building's true value, which is at least ten times as much, but
which is the Ecclesiastical Insurance Office's assessment of the
maximum amount of damage which is likely to be caused in
any one incident. A cathedral may be dedicated to an unseen
spirit, and more often than not a long-dead saint as well, but
to function effectively it needs drain cleaners, environmental
health officers and steeplejacks, plumbers and stonemasons, fire
chiefs and building inspectors, just as much as bishops, deans
and canons. For such people a cathedral definitely is *not* a
mystery. Indeed, it would be alarming – in the case of an
electrician, say, or an organ tuner – if it were. For such people
a cathedral is a down-to-earth construction of stone, timber,
lead and glass relying on human knowledge and skill for its
preservation. In one sense it is, as the Bruckner anthem puts
it,[6] built by God: in another, it most definitely is not. Most of
the master craftsman who directed building works from the

fourteenth century onwards are recorded, and all but a handful of the later architects and craftsmen are known, as are the cathedral architects, engineers and quantity surveyors of today: real people erecting, repairing and developing real buildings. As Bishop Aurelio says to Blaise Meredith in *The Devil's Advocate*, 'If reason and revelation mean anything they mean that a man works out his salvation in the body by the use of material things'.[7]

One of the questions over which argument rages is the way in which the material body of the cathedral – its walls, roofs, windows and contents – should be treated. When does a piece of masonry, or a lead sheet, or a stained-glass panel, reach the point where it must be repaired, and how far-reaching should the repairs be? Wall paintings and medieval glass are particularly sensitive subjects. Bearing in mind that a historic building does not decay uniformly and that one badly eroded stone may be surrounded by several others which could last another 30 or 40 years, how extensive should the new work be? In his 1877 manifesto for the Society for the Protection of Ancient Buildings, William Morris recommended 'staving off decay by daily care' but 'otherwise to resist all tampering with either the fabric or ornament of the building as it stands'. On the other hand, the British Standard *Guide to the Principles of the Conservation of Historic Buildings*, while stating that minimum intervention is fundamental to good conservation, concedes that 'if, for example, it should be necessary to provide scaffold access to a high or otherwise inaccessible part of a building, it may be sensible to carry out more repairs to that part of the building than were strictly necessary at the time'.[8] Are increased scaffolding costs a price worth paying for maintaining the weather-beaten surface of an ageing building which fascinates historians, artists and archaeologists alike? The same question can be asked about invasive engineering works designed to arrest structural movement. I doubt there are many today who would see cathedrals turned into museums rather than adapted to modern use, but major historic components can still be irretrievably lost. It is only comparatively recently that the medieval roof timbers above the vaulting at Norwich were replaced with steel and concrete trusses, and it was fear of irreversible damage which fuelled the controversies over the great West Door at York and the floors at Chester. The removal of worn stone paving is a particularly delicate subject, as it loses its picturesque character when it is relaid for safety reasons or for the installation of underfloor heating, but there can be compensatory archaeological discoveries. Saxon walls and twelfth-century burials were found at Chester, and the remains of St Wilfrid's church have been unearthed at Ripon. When, where and how far to dig is as important a question as when and how to repair.

One reason why cathedrals are, at times, an architectural battleground could be that, whatever the original explanation for them, there is no general agreement these days about what they are for. The large number of people who have an interest in their well-being inevitably causes tension because the needs of the shareholders conflict. Cathedrals mean different things to different people, all of whom feel they have a stake in their continued existence. For some – stonemasons, glaziers and architects for instance (not to mention the armies of flower arrangers, bell ringers, vergers, librarians, shop assistants, organists and administrators) – the explanation is simple: cathedrals are a source of rewarding employment and fulfil-ment, often for many years. For archaeologists and art historians, cathedrals are an equally absorbing study as, in spite of the research work of the last 100 years, there is still a great deal which is not known about them. But what about the people who see them as places not just to study and wander about in, but to worship in and *use*? How easy are cathedrals to visit if you are in some way disadvantaged or have fallen foul of society? How accessible are they to people without money? How do you explain the art and architecture to the blind, the liturgy and music to the deaf? What if you are in a wheelchair? Most important of all, what if you are a bereaved visitor who just wants a quiet place in which to be counselled or to weep? For all their size, few cathedrals have spaces where it is possible to be silent, and in the future such sound-proof enclosures may have to be built.

Fresh thinking is possible in other areas. Advances in sound reinforcement technology, for example, have done away with the need for towering pulpits and umbrella-like testers, while the importance now given to the Body and body language in Christian thinking has led to a new need to see and be seen, and to touch and be touched in the Peace at the Eucharist. Experiments in drawing near to each other involve fresh, often radical, approaches to seating. From a liturgical point of view, the ideal cathedral today would probably be a large square or circular hall, like the Church of the Reconciliation at Taizé, or Alison and Peter Smithson's unsuccessful Coventry design, with spaces and fittings which can be used by different denominations, perhaps indeed different faiths, and where everything is movable so that experiments can be conducted rapidly at little or no cost. The reality is that liturgical innovation, not to mention the secular uses to which cathedrals are put, has to take place in narrow stone corridors where vision and movement is impaired by thick columns and impenetrable screens, in many cases dividing one end of the building from the other. It is, for many, an irksome constraint and it is not just those immediately responsible for the building who can feel frustrated. The modern worshipper, tourist and pilgrim look these days for lavatories (there were none at Norwich or St Albans until a few years ago), nappy-changing facilities, cafeterias serving refreshments, stalls with books and guides, shops with mugs and CDs and cathedral marmalade, explanatory TV displays, wheelchair ramps for the disabled, aids for the blind, guard rails to protect high-level walkways and galleries, and doors and exit signs to ensure safe evacuation in the event of fire. All these involve conspicuous visual changes to the time-honoured walls and floors.

To add to the problem of how something so solid, so seemingly intractable, can evolve and adapt in response to changing needs and to developments in the way we communicate with each other, English Heritage has its own agenda, putting the brakes on what can and cannot be done: a state-appointed watchdog of the nation's treasures in the tense alliance between conservationists and innovators, which it is the duty of the Cathedrals Fabric Commission for England (CFCE) to prevent from becoming a contest. The objectives of the CFCE are, first, 'To help ensure that our cathedrals are cared for and conserved to the highest possible standards; such that public confidence may be maintained in the Church of England's responsible stewardship of these buildings, which have a pre-eminent place in the nation's heritage and identity'; and secondly, 'to balance the requirements of conservation with the need for our cathedrals to continue and develop their proper role as the seat of the diocesan bishop and as a centre of Christian worship and mission'.[9] The interests represented on the CFCE could not be more wide-ranging: the General Synod, the House of Bishops, the Deans' and Provosts' Conference, the Liturgical Commission, the Council for the Care of Churches, the Ecclesiastical Architects and Surveyors Association, the Institutions of Structural and of Civil Engineers, the Royal Academy of Art, the Royal School of Church Music, the Royal Fine Art Commission, the Society of Antiquaries, the Council for British Archaeology, English Heritage and the Secretary of State for the Environment. Moreover at diocesan (Fabric Advisory Committee) level, not only are notices of intent served on the local planning authority, but five national amenity societies are notified of changes as well: the Ancient Monuments Society, the Victorian Society, the Georgian Group, the Civic Trust and the Thirties Society. It would be hard to devise stronger armour to protect cathedrals from poorly thought-out alterations, or indeed a more inclusive group of expert interests. The problem is that, while failure can be filtered out, it does not guarantee excellence or even success, any more than the British Standard Guide can produce architects with sensitivity and imagination. The CFCE can only arbitrate – it cannot dictate what is done – nor can the British Standards Institute nor English Heritage. The future development of cathedrals depends in the end on the ability – the will – of deans and provosts and their chapters to spot and encourage outstanding talent which, in turn, has the best chance of flourishing if they are outstandingly talented themselves.

How to promote the best and prevent the worst, how to introduce the new without ruining the old: these are the vital questions facing cathedrals today. We have highly developed techniques for dismantling and reassembling priceless artefacts, if only for repair, and equally sophisticated methods for recording historic treasures. The problem in the past has not been the removal of important screens, galleries and glass but their subsequent destruction. Provided safe, long-term storage can be found in the empty roof spaces and store rooms with which cathedrals and their precincts usually abound, there is no reason why quite substantial parts of the fabric cannot be removed, if that is needed to prevent the cathedral's vital arteries from becoming clogged. Conservation does not mean keeping things as they are, setting them in aspic, but the avoidance of irreparable damage. Buildings are not exempt from the process of decaying and dying. Cathedrals, like us, are affected by the passage of time, not just through the tramp of tourists' feet but by the chemical reaction of limestone with carbon dioxide in rain, and by atmospheric pollution. 'There's no cure for death', Carlo Rienzi tells Peter Landon in *Daughter of Silence*, 'but there is a high art in its deferment.'[10] Meanwhile, is it fear of the future, or of the ugliness of the new, or is it a feeling of guilt and remorse which is behind our resistance to change? Perhaps it is a recognition that, with the widespread destruction of historic buildings and cities in the last 90 years – along with the contamination of rivers and the decimation of the nation's wildlife and the natural habitat – our stock of the material things which give life purpose and meaning is finite, like the Earth itself.

The cathedral conservation movement is fuelled by a determination to prevent further losses and irreversible architectural damage in the pursuit of what could prove to be short-lived liturgical fashion. Today, stylistic innovation in architecture is occurring at an ever-increasing rate and there is no general agreement as to what that style should be, but this volatile situation and cultural flux is a great opportunity for the Church of England which, institutionally and theologically, seems built to cope creatively with change. It is important, however, that the CFCE exists to be the referee on what can and cannot be matters for experiment. It is often said that conservationists want to turn church buildings into museums where heritage experiences replace worship and other intimations of the divine. This is not so; indeed it is vital for the well-being of cathedrals that their development is monitored with care. English Heritage is understandably opposed to irreversible damage because that is what has happened to cathedrals in the past, resulting in serious loss of the nation's treasures. No reasonable conservationist, however, aware of being on common ground shared by many others, can object to careful alterations where vital fabric is not lost. As for liturgical innovation, it seems to me that quite major experiments can be conducted, provided that what is done is reversible and nothing is destroyed. Given expertise, care and long-term storage space there is no reason why large intractable objects like stone pulpits and altar rails cannot be dismantled and stored, if that is liturgically important; why even glazing cannot be removed and placed in racks for a few years. A surprising amount of fabric *can* be altered reversibly. At St Albans, the large Victorian nave pulpit was taken down in the 1970s and replaced with a wood-panelled preaching box from a Norfolk country church, resting on castors so that it can be pushed aside for concerts (or, as happened once, wheeled out of sight by a quick-thinking verger when a protester climbed into it during a service in order to harangue the congregation). At Ely and elsewhere, the nave choir stalls are movable too.

The English are at their best living in – and fighting their way out of – a muddle, adjusting to a world where there are no ideal solutions. We should not be afraid of making reversible mistakes, especially as 'reversible' is a word enshrined in the British Standard Institute's guide. The atrophied character of some recent cathedral alterations and additions could be due to a perception that everything which is new must be as permanent as the enclosing walls and vaulting. This view must change: architects, artists and craftsmen – and donors in particular – must accept that they cannot be given guarantees that their work will be on indefinite display. They are at best participants (perhaps only briefly) in the life of an ever-changing organism. The Church of today is not a rock of ages: it is rather a ship at sea in lively motion. It would be overdramatic to describe cathedrals as a battleground: the differing parties are too civilised for that. A better analogy would be a tug-of-war where the rope is circular not straight, with people pulling at various points on the circumference which, if anyone tugs too hard, becomes an unsightly, shapeless loop. How to hold the circle – how to keep the parties around the edge respectful of each other – is the architectural challenge facing cathedrals today. The omens for success are good.

SEVEN

JEWELS IN THE DUST

Art in cathedrals

KEITH WALKER

Some months ago a disconsolate middle-aged woman wandered into Winchester Cathedral. She might have resorted to her parish priest or to a friend, but she needed the sacred space of a cathedral church. Recently she had been bereaved, and life seemed hard and confused. In the north transept she paused beneath a 5.5-foot wooden sculpture of the crucifixion by Peter Eugene Ball. As she spent time gazing at this object in this environment, her black mood was dissipated and she redis-covered integration with God and life. Such experiences, in greater or lesser intensity, may not be rare. They remind us of why cathedrals are built and suggest the power of their form and contents.

In an unpublished address Bishop J. V. Taylor has suggested that cathedrals are shrines. A shrine, according to the origin of the word, is a box or chest containing a precious object or objects. Most of us think of shrines as holy places where the relics of a saint may be found. At Westminster Abbey or Hereford Cathedral we encounter the remains of such shrines, and we notice that the edifice reflects in some measure the quality of the material within. Medieval shrines were tradition-ally beautifully coloured and sculpted, celebrating both the saint and the doctrines of the Christian religion. In addition, shrines are places to which people come on pilgrimage. To be near the relics of the saint is to be near the spot of infective holiness. It is a place of prayer.

The bare cathedral building houses the liturgy, which reaches its consummation in the celebration of the Eucharist. In addition, the cathedral is the seat of the bishop, who focuses he unity of the diocese. He represents the meeting-point of the local diocese and the whole Catholic Church, in time and across the world. He represents the teaching authority of that Church. The cathedral building should reflect in shape and decoration these two cardinal points respecting the liturgy and the office of the bishop. If we visit a great cathedral, such as Chartres, we can experience a magnificent realisation of this understanding. Here the visual and theological perceptions are united, and each is a sophisticated achievement. The spires of Chartres can be seen from miles away over the surrounding plain. They signal the presence of an important building, and their shape represents visibly the aspiration of prayer. The cathedral is entered at the west. Highly sculpted tympanums, and other sculptures, announce to the pilgrim the significance of this great edifice. Over the Royal Portal we find Christ in majesty surrounded by the four Evangelists, symbolised by the biblical images of the man, the lion, the ox and the eagle. Immediately inside the cathedral, pilgrims realise that they have passed a threshold of consciousness: the architectural shapes, the volumes of space and, most of all, the effect of the stained glass, tell them that they stand in sacred space, while previously they stood in profane space. The ground plan is cruciform, and the font is near the west door: thus progress through the cathedral is a walking of the path of salvation. The progressive themes of the stained-glass windows interpret the pilgrims' walk, as they move eastwards towards their desti-nation, kneeling eventually near the enshrined tunicle of the Blessed Virgin Mary. For true pilgrims, the unfolding of the cathedral before their eyes as they walk will have been accompanied by the unfolding of their inner selves.

Visitors to a great English cathedral today – say Canterbury or Durham – are unlikely to discover what our medieval forebears experienced. Two related factors explain this: the depredations of history and the changed psyche of modern Europeans. The Reformation, which erupted in the sixteenth century, but which extended, with intermissions until 1660, altered the nature of Christian belief in England in important respects. The sense of continuity between Bible and Church tradition was broken and the Bible was granted overwhelming authority in determining Christian belief (although this belief did go through various developments). Bible reading, listening to the Bible being read in worship, and the act of preaching (which was understood to be the exposition of the Bible and its application), were given paramount importance. Thus, the sense of hearing and the act of speech were primary, whereas the sense of sight depreciated in importance. Salvation was deemed to be by faith, and faith was an individual, heartfelt response to the word. Thus the sacramental system of the medieval Church was undercut, with all that that meant in terms of the importance of the church building, the liturgy and the priest.

The Reformers took the second commandment, enunciated in Exodus 20, very seriously. Graven images were to be prohibited. Since the pre-Reformation Church had tried to educate its largely illiterate adherents by pictorial means, and that Church was now regarded as heretical, images became doubly abhorrent, and objects of suspicion. The belief developed that, as the early Church became accepted in the world in the fourth century, images had become part of its life. Beauty, associated with worldly possessions and women, was a further aggravating cause leading to the condemnation of images. Fuel was added to this fire by the politics of Henry VIII and some of his successors, and by class grievance. The great cathedrals found themselves largely denuded of stained glass, statuary, shrines, textiles, precious metal, paintings, and similar manifestations of a religion largely dependent both on the sense of sight and a Catholic form of belief. In the BBC television series *History of British Art* (1996), Andrew Graham Dixon extolled the battered and deformed sculpture of Christ, carved just before the Reformation, dislodged and abused presumably at the Reformation, and accidentally found buried beneath the site of the Mercers' Chapel in London in 1954. He said that it was one of the most magnificent sculptures he had ever seen, and pondered the wound to our culture, inflicted by Reforming zeal, which has yet to heal. There have been religious and secular barriers to that much-needed healing process.

The Reformation was followed by the Enlightenment. The late seventeenth century and the eighteenth century was predominantly a period when Protestant culture prevailed, and an increasing emphasis was put upon technical, as against intuitive, reason. It was the time of common sense, the disparaging of tradition, and of experiment. The work of Newton encouraged the notion of light as a cultural emblem. Churches were whitewashed and plain glass was held to admit the honest light of God's day. While the Romantic movement and Tractarianism challenged many of these assumptions, as the nineteenth century proceeded, industrialisation made a further onslaught on tradition and the nurturing of sacred beauty. The twentieth century has experienced the retreat from religious observance and the growth of commercialism as a cultural paradigm. None of these movements, apart from Romanticism and Tractarianism, has helped to heal the aesthetic and religious wounds in our culture. Blake's dictum that empire follows art, and not art empire, as Englishmen suppose, must seem as odd a remark today as when the great visionary first made it.

To write about the balance in the human psyche in different historical periods is a hazardous undertaking, but the form we attribute to a period of civilisation, and the kind of philosophical writing of a period, must give expression to the particular way in which people experience life in a specific period. Everyone would agree, for example, that medieval people tended to be theistic, as modern people tend to be secular. Everyone would agree that art held a place in medieval society that it does not hold today: then it was central; now it is decorative and peripheral. Granted that previous period's rootedness in nature and our deracination, adherence to the deliberations of technical reason, and commercial life, the experience of Darwin, described by Aldous Huxley, must seem to have general application:

> One-pointed concentration on that which is not the highest may become a dangerous form of idolatry. In a letter to Hooker, Darwin wrote that 'it is a cursed evil to any man to become so absorbed in any subject as I am in mine.' It is an evil because such one-pointedness may result in the more or less total atrophy of all but one side of the mind. Darwin himself records that in later life he was unable to take the smallest interest in poetry, art or religion.[1]

Where our seeing tends to be plain, the seeing of medieval humanity tended to be in-sight, a seeing into. The medievals commonly distinguished four ascending dimensions in the act of seeing, whether of a text or something other than visual. There was the literal – as Jan van Eyck's fifteenth-century painting of the Virgin and Child might represent a woman and child. There was the allegorical – as the painting might represent the Church who offers Christ. There was the moral – as the painting might represent my humility before this ever-present allegorical reality. There was the anagogical – as the painting might represent my experience of salvation. In this painting it is significant that the donor, Canon George Stolz, kneels before the Virgin and Child, book in hand but spectacles clasped in the other hand. His physical eyes cannot see and do not need to see, as he is beholding a vision. He sees with the eye of his heart. As for us, we must recognise that we are as we are. Together with acknowledging the benefits of living in our particular culture, we must heed the warning that we might have developed psychically in a lop-sided manner. We must be careful of one-pointed concentration, and must expose ourselves to those influences that sensitise and develop aesthetic and sacred awareness. While art historical, liturgical and theological knowledge are all-important for the person who would nurture the appropriate care and embellishment of our cathedrals, sensitive awareness of form and colour and their symbolic import are of prime significance. I have indicated elsewhere that Church of England theological colleges and Roman Catholic seminaries do not generally give the appropriate importance in priestly formation to this type of education,[2] and the present unsatisfactory situation will only improve as those who lead the Church at local and national levels understand and see the importance of the visual in ecclesiological terms.

～◦～

We proceed now to Anglican cathedrals in England as we find them. We inherit them at a particular point in their history. They number 44, if we include Westminster Abbey. Certain churches have been elevated to cathedral status since the Reformation, but all of these buildings are pre-Reformation in origin except the cathedrals of Liverpool, Coventry, Guildford, London and Truro. That is to say that a Catholic culture gave almost all our cathedrals their form. Those cathedrals built since the Reformation draw powerfully on that Catholic tradition, and it is difficult to see how a strong Protestant conviction can honour and embellish them. We have only to visit Calvinist Holland to experience the truth of this assertion. The original structures of St Bavo's Church, Haarlem, St John's

The lantern of St Nicholas's Cathedral, Newcastle. Romantic images of cathedrals forget that often these great ecclesiastical buildings stand at the heart of large industrial cities. They help focus the aspirations and the fears of the communities they serve.

(Photograph © Leslie Garland Picture Library.)

[left] Norwich – Bishop's Throne. Right up in the apse of the presbytery is the ancient bishop's throne, reflecting the practice of former times even when it was installed just before 1100; it looks back to the pattern of the Roman basilica. The bishop was flanked by his 'family' (*familia*).
(Photograph courtesy of the Dean and Chapter of Norwich Cathedral.)

[below] Liverpool interior. Liverpool was designed before the advent of new patterns for worship. Nevertheless the sheer majesty of the great central space and nave bridge offer enormous opportunities for the variety of liturgies for which cathedrals are now used.
(Photograph courtesy of the Dean and Chapter of Liverpool Cathedral.)

[above] Ely – 'the Ship of the Fens'. Originally an actual island, Ely breathes a sense of mystery and magnificence in the heart of the fens. Here travellers have received counsel or sustenance from the Benedictine monks who were responsible for the cathedral.
(Photograph © Geoff Newman.)

[right] Winchester – *Christus* by Peter Eugene Ball (1987). Cathedrals have, throughout the centuries, been patrons of the arts. A balance between clear theological symbolism and true art is one of the issues central to commissioning.
(Photograph courtesy of the Dean and Chapter of Winchester Cathedral.)

York – the nave. York's Gothic nave is a fine example of how space in a cathedral can offer people an experience unavailable in other buildings, due to the capacity to evoke transcendence.

(Photograph courtesy of the Friends of York Minster.)

Church, s'Hertogensbosch, and the Old Church, Amsterdam, are in conflict with present usage. Restoration and embellishment have proved an indifferent achievement. The difficulty of Protestantism with Catholic-type buildings is understandable: it springs from theological roots, coloured by a particular history. Anglicanism prides itself on being both Catholic and Reformed, and the ambiguity of our heritage explains why our care and embellishment of cathedrals varies both from epoch to epoch and between particular dioceses.

In face of the Protestant challenge, a brief defence of the Catholic-type understanding of cathedrals runs as follows. The building houses the liturgy, which finds its normative expression in the celebration of the Eucharist. The form of the building and its furnishings is a response to this awesome fact. The significant features of the cathedral must support and interpret the Eucharist, but this principle should not be too narrowly or rigorously practised. The principle will embrace the recognition that, as the mother church of the diocese, the cathedral should be large and the processional ways spacious. The cathedral is the seat of the bishop, and music is an important auditory support for the liturgy. The structure must take account of this. The cathedral will be visited by tourists and pilgrims – a shrine has an inevitable centripetal effect; so care must be taken in furnishings to take account of such guests. At the theological level, we will surely wish to interpret the meaning of the Eucharist broadly. Creation matters as well as redemption; the cosmos as well as the earth; eternity as well as time. The distance a particular sculpture stands from the altar, for example, may well suggest different kinds of propriety. A crucifix may well stand near the altar, an abstract image suggestive of the divine energy flowing through created things may be more appropriately sited in the nave or crypt.

At this point something more should be said about the meaning of sacred visual art. It is intended to please, as its expression fulfils aesthetic norms, and humankind both creates and responds to aesthetic reality. In addition it is intended to instruct. Pope Leo the Great (died 461) established the view that the image was the Bible of the poor. The illiterate could understand visual forms, even if they could not read, and they could learn God's truth in this way. Both these points are significant today. Aesthetics is important, and in support of this we can refer to the growing numbers of visitors to art galleries and cathedrals. Those visiting cathedrals, however, are likely to have a very superficial understanding of the Christian religion. Despite a now far more general literacy, Pope Leo's dictum has an extended meaning today. We live no longer in a biblical culture – but sacred visual art takes us beyond this. The creation of the great artist runs alongside statements fashioned in words and logic. It has its own verbally inexpressible truth and power to enter into dialogue with the beholders for the transformation of their understanding and emotions.

Traditionally it has been understood that there are three absolute values – goodness, beauty and truth. These values are rooted in God and express the divine nature and purpose. According to the purity of the perception, higher and lower manifestations of these values may be recognised. They are called values because they are subject to qualitative judgements: they cannot be measured or given quantitative equivalents. We participate in them according to the level of our spiritual growth. They can be distinguished but not separated; and they cannot be separated from God. Experience of them may well bring religious conviction to a person. The Christian Platonist, Dean Inge, proposed these criteria for their discernment:

> First, they are not means to something else, nor even to each other, though they are not sundered from each other, but united in a threefold cord not quickly broken. Next, they have a universal quality. They take us out of ourselves, out of the small circle of our private personal

interests. In a sense, they are essentially impersonal. Lastly, they satisfy, delight, and elevate us, so that when we have been in contact with them we feel that we have found our highest or deepest selves.[3]

Visual art in cathedrals may be religious as it celebrates the dogmas of our religion; spiritual as, with or without the religious element, it expresses an intensity of life; and sacred as, once more, with or without the religious, it is sacramental, communicating the energy of God to the beholder.

Art in the West has tended to be representational. In the East, however, channelled by Orthodoxy, sacramental art has flourished. Philip Sherrard elucidates the art of the icon thus:

> There is here no distinction between art and contemplation. The artist must raise his vision from earthly to divine concerns and perceptions until he can mentally entertain the form which he is to imitate – until this form lives within him with its own inherent vitality. There has to be an endless renewal and repetition of the internal imaginative act, an endless recreation within the life of the artist of the spiritual realities which are the subject of his work, and which must spontaneously inform his work if it is to live. The iconographic form – the ascertained rules of the art – are simply the means spontaneously assumed by these realities in order to express themselves.[4]

Sherrard uses the same reasoning to expound the creation of Orthodox churches – their building and their decoration, understood as a unit. The overall shape is archetypal, and its decoration in fresco and icon reflects this. The life of heaven is painted in the upper domed area, with Christ Pantocrator (ruler of all) in the highest and central point. Biblical scenes and the story of salvation occupy the middle zones. Saints and martyrs, and the life of the Church on earth, occupy the ground level.

This view of the function of sacred visual artists clearly elevates their work to something akin to that of the prophet. This would not have surprised the leaders of the Romantic movement. Coleridge puts it in his own way:

> The imagination, then, I consider either as primary, or secondary. The primary imagination I hold to be the living power and prime agent of all human perception, and as a repetition in the finite mind of the eternal act of creation in the infinite I AM. The secondary imagination I consider as an echo of the former, co-existing with the conscious will, yet still as identical with the primary in the kind of its agency, and differing only in degree, and in the mode of its operation. It dissolves, diffuses, dissipates in order to re-create; or where this process is rendered impossible, yet still at all events it struggles to idealise and unify. It is essentially vital, even as all objects (as objects) are essentially fixed and dead. Fancy, on the contrary, has no other counters to play with, but fixities and definites ... Equally with the ordinary memory the Fancy must receive all its materials ready made from the law of association.[5]

Such views, and indeed the long tradition of the Catholic Church, help us to respond to the incipient Protestantism and secular functionalism that infects much Anglican thought. This thought was the scaffolding of *Heritage and Renewal* (1995), the Archbishops' Commission Report on the role and function of cathedrals today. Its pages contain much useful practical advice on administration and finance. A chapter is given to cathedral music, but scarcely a paragraph is devoted to visual art. The theological problem is focused in the second Mosaic commandment, which should not be absolutised but interpreted historically: fighting for the integrity of their own belief, the Israelites understandably condemned neighbouring religions, which sometimes seduced Israelites. Images, however, are usually regarded as means of contemplation, or vehicles through which the divine may be encountered. The educated have never confused the image with its prototype. Secondly, the incarnation was the enfleshing of God: deity was present on earth, and its artistic representation can scarcely be condemned. The Catholic tradition also gives credit to the imaginative and creative abilities of humankind. Such a view exalts the capacity of humanity as created in the image of God and as able to be God's co-worker. However real the Fall is held to be, and however much sin is believed to debase humanity, such glorious capacities are safeguarded. Entailed in such a view is the recognition that God is immanent as well as transcendent. This type of thinking undergirds sacramental teaching that honours the real presence in the Eucharist, and finds 'memorialism' inadequate.

In the context of our own perceptions, we enter our cathedrals and find them to be sacred space and fitting representations of the Kingdom of Heaven. They are engines for the transformation of the inner life of humankind, and their focus is the Eucharist. The conservation of their decoration, in the age of the Cathedrals' Measure (1990), is in good hands. Neglect or vandalism by deans and chapters, who have authority for the cathedral day by day, is likely to be checked. The Fabric Advisory Committee supplies a local panel of persons expert in different fields pertinent to the life and fabric of cathedrals. The Cathedrals Fabric Commission for England is a national co-ordinating body to which complex or controversial matters may be referred. I have argued elsewhere that the new controls are inevitable, granted the national effort to conserve our heritage.[6] I have also argued that good, even excellent, work is done in conservation, but that difficulties may arise where new visual embellishment is envisaged – and I mention cases that illustrate my argument. Here is another case in point.

While Sherborne Abbey counts as a parish church, and so comes under the supervision of the Diocesan Advisory Committee and the Council for the Care of Churches, nevertheless the principles are very similar to those involved in cathedrals, especially since Sherborne Abbey must rank as an ancient ecclesiastical building of the first rank. The vicar, church-wardens, parochial church council, and church architect all wished to replace the great West Window with a new creation. The existing West Window was designed by A. W. Pugin in 1851, and was made into glass and inserted by Hardman. It seems that Hardman underfired the glass. Certainly the colour leached from the serried ranks of saints and patriarchs and, by 1989, a new window of quality was required. The design proposed by John Hayward had the advantage of focusing on the Blessed Virgin Mary – to whom the abbey is dedicated – and on the Christ Child. At first the Council for the Care of Churches supported the scheme but later, when the Victorian Society lodged an objection, joined the opposition. The opposition was determined, but so were the abbey representatives. Lawrence Lee, sometime head of the department of stained glass at the Royal College of Art, made a submission on behalf of the parish with these words:

> Over the years there has risen an army of experts whose efforts in many fields I would unreservedly commend, but now, growing ever more intrusive into the work of Diocese and Parish, have tended to defend poor quality works purely because they have historical rather than artistic importance. Inevitably this has led to regarding churches as museums rather than living communities.

The Revd Dr Allan Doig, formerly university lecturer in the history and theory of art at the University of Kent, made this observation in his deposition:

> Works of art have 'life' to the extent that they resonate

with other works of art in close proximity to them in time or space, and with others to which they refer. More importantly, perhaps, is that we recognise that they have life when they resonate with our own lives and the lives of many within (and beyond) the community to which they belong ... Sherborne Abbey ... can ... be likened to a palimpsest with many generations of erasures and rewritings revivifying the story being told.

The court representative of the Council for the Care of Churches told the *Sunday Telegraph*: 'There is no artist I could confidently recommend to do a window in a church of any quality – if I were asked by a parish, I'd suggest that they spend their money some other way.'[7]

After much heartache, and expenditure of time and money, the Court of Arches, in 1996, found in favour of the vicar of Sherborne, but the parish had to pay the costs of the appeal. The director of the Victorian Society and the secretary of the Council for the Care of Churches declared themselves very disappointed with the outcome, but intimated that they were unlikely to make a final appeal to the Privy Council.[8]

The reasons why supervisory committees sometimes have a distorted perception of fine old churches can now be stated. First, our culture is more sympathetic to the reassurances of the old than the challenges of the new. Artistic experimentation in the course of the twentieth century has had ambiguous results. Some of the innovators have also tended to disparage tradition. Our culture is currently compensating for this by exalting the old and being wary of the new. It is both amusing and tragic to note that those who safeguard the medieval achievement often resist the medieval spirit in face of innovation. Almost any great old church will provide numerous examples of our distant forebears destroying good art and architecture for the sake of the new. The north and south transepts of Winchester Cathedral, for example, suggest that the original nave must have been a fine sight, but the new style of Gothic remodelled the existing Romanesque nave in the fourteenth century. Secondly, the undoubted skills of the majority of members of supervisory committees are largely practical, historical and conservationist. It is no surprise that the secretary of the Council for the Care of Churches is a member of the executive committee of the Victorian Society, and that the secretary of the Cathedrals Fabric Commission for England was trained as an archaeologist. Thirdly, committees tend by their very nature to compromise and are more at ease with what is habitual than with risk. Fourthly, the supervisory committees know that there are those in our society who would like old churches to come under ordinary statutory control. Such knowledge makes them vulnerable to the representations of the amenity societies – voluntary bodies such as the Victorian Society, which are pressure groups working for the conservation of our heritage, understood in particular ways.

All of this means that deans and chapters must emulate the spirit of the vicar of Sherborne and his parochial church council. They should resist the views and overriding power of expert opinion, which we can recognise often to be biased. The assertion, for example, that there is no glass-maker worthy of a major commission at Sherborne Abbey is simply ridiculous. How can it be that the secretary of the Council for the Care of Churches cannot respond to the Holy Spirit Window at All Saints' Church, Basingstoke, designed by Cecil Collins and made by Patrick Reyntiens? Or the East Window at Salisbury Cathedral, made by Gabriel Loire? Or the Baptistry Window created by Brian Young for St John's Church, Johannesburg? Or the Last Supper stained-glass window by Mark Angus in Durham Cathedral? Such a list of artists engaged in exemplary practice is by no means exhaustive; but it is sufficient to indicate the difficulty that those involved in new creation have with established authority.

Something must be said, in conclusion, about new work in our old cathedrals. Much of what is said will apply with modification to the creation of sacred visual art in any context. First, the aspiration must be for excellence. Any church, as a house of God, should have this aspiration – but a cathedral, as the mother church of the diocese and the seat of the bishop, is required especially so to aspire. From many years spent in commissioning art for churches, my impression is that there are artists available for any commission, but they must be selected carefully. It may be that they have little or no ecclesiastical experience. What they create determines their value. Since the Reformation there has been an estrangement between visual art and the Church. Even the Roman Catholic Church has grown defensive and is liable to confuse Renaissance-type forms with appropriateness. If the Church is serious about mission, however, and if it lives by faith (which Paul Tillich was prepared to interpret as risk), then it must seek to embrace artists with their own iconographical forms. There is nothing finally determinative about artistic form in the fifteen and sixteenth centuries. Artists of integrity will inevitably use creative forms natural to them because of the cultural milieu in which they live. The Church should dictate the subject matter, the artist the treatment. Furthermore, if the Church itself is contemporary, it will long for the reinterpretations which present-day artists will give to ancient themes.

Recently, for example, I was asked to advise the dean and chapter of a certain cathedral about an artist to create a painting for a significant space within the cathedral. I suggested Robert Natkin, an American abstract expressionist, most of whose work seems to me to be both of high artistic merit and sacred in intensity. Immediately discussion became difficult, and one large church-funding body was said to be very unlikely to be interested in helping. My mind went back to Dean Inge (who was quoted appreciatively above) as typifying an attitude far too common in the Church today, when he wrote, in 1933:

As for the deliberate ugliness of much modernist sculpture and painting, I can only regard it as a disease, and hope that the evil fashion will soon pass away. It aims, we are told, at 'expressiveness', disregarding all accepted standards of beauty. Unfortunately, what it expresses is barbarous and repulsive. There may be some geometric art, as Spinoza gave us a geometric ethics. But the whole movement is absurd, or would be if it were not connected with the horrors of Bolshevist materialism.[9]

Inge doubtless had in mind such artists as Epstein, Moore, Hepworth, Matisse, Chagall, Braque, Rouault and Le Corbusier, who produced some of the most important sacred art of our century. But Inge, one of the most distinguished churchmen of his day, presumably reviled everything they created.

Any new work introduced into an existing cathedral must be contextually right. This is not a question of using identical idioms of expression: at Winchester Cathedral, for example, we have Romanesque, Gothic (in its different phases), and Classical styles intermingling one with the other. The harmony of the whole comes from excellence in quality, and from new artists, over the centuries, having visualised their work *in situ* before creating it. There is, furthermore, an interest and wholesomeness in some situations of experiencing aesthetic interruption and change. Harmony and homogeneity may be dull.

We must also recognise that many works of art die with time. Wear and tear is one reason for this. English cathedrals have passed through the traumas of the Reformation and Civil War, and the centuries of neglect consequent upon a Protestant ascendancy. Another reason is that paintings and textiles may well fade in the sun, sculpture may crack through alterations in temperature; in the course of centuries, stained glass tends to lose the vitality of its colour. A time must therefore come when what is born in time is allowed to die in time. We may conserve what is good from the past, seeing in such conservation piety towards our ancestors, continuity through history, and an admiration for works that transcend immediate time and speak to our condition. What happened in the case of a local congregation at Sherborne, however, suggests that the conserving mentality is not held in judicious balance with other factors, in the minds and emotions of those who have power to assist or hinder the visual life of our cathedrals. Surely Dr Allan Doig was right, in the case of Sherborne, to say that great old buildings must be understood as palimpsests. The word has its primary reference in relation to documents which include erasures and new additions. Our great old cathedrals are like this too. But the prevailing historicist dogma clouds enthusiasm and often obstructs the path of those who would appropriately erase in order to write again, clearly and well.

The value of the addition of appropriate new work to an existing cathedral is in making the cathedral's statement more complete. Something is added that was not there before. It allows our generation to speak to our generation. Theology as a verbal and logical discipline moves on. Culture itself moves on. The Blessed Virgin Mary meant one kind of person in medieval times, another kind of person now. Obedience and chastity do not mean for us what they meant centuries ago. Nor can we think, as Michelangelo did, that Mary's youthful beauty was maintained throughout her life. Nor does a democratic mentality so honour aristocratic habits that Mary's form should be thought rightly modelled according to aristocratic precedent. What applies to the image of Mary applies to most images in cathedrals. Cathedrals are a meeting-point between Church and world. What we display there should be what we believe. Lastly, in the course of new work being commissioned and realised, relationships are built up between the commissioning body and particular artists. Such a process helps to heal the cultural wound between the artistic and ecclesiastical establishments. That our cathedrals and churches need such healing has been the burden of this essay. When we think of the art of Gilbert and George, Damien Hirst and Francis Bacon, we see that art is no autonomous venture, and that the redemptive element in Christianity could help to heal the cultural wound in art.

In the 1970s Dean Sidney Evans recognised the impoverished state of most of his cathedral textiles at Salisbury. He was able to engage the talent and energy of Jane Lemon, who had worked in the theatre, to develop a team of proficient textile-workers to renew cathedral textiles, so that Salisbury Cathedral has become a centre for textile renewal in the diocese and beyond. The principle involved here is one we ought to heed. The renewal of sacred visual art needs seeds of life from which growth can more generally come. It may be that people with a knowledge of the arts and with proven insight should be appointed to the staffs of our cathedrals. It may be that a visual arts officer should be appointed in the diocese to advise on such matters. It may be that an appointment of a textile artist along the lines of Salisbury should be instituted. Such developments would indicate the seriousness with which the Church would be taking this dimension of its ministry. We must all look forward to the day when the keenness and discrimination that marks conservation of the visual in our cathedrals is spread to the nobler ideal of appropriate embellishment, to the glory of God and the joy of humankind.

EIGHT

LOCUS ISTE[1]

Cathedral theology

STEPHEN PLATTEN

Sir Gilbert [Lewis] . . . said mad people are apt to come to Cathedrals. There was a mad woman who came to Worcester Cathedral and gave him a great deal of trouble by screeching out. There was a Mr Quarrell who used to make antics at the time of the Communion. At a certain point in the service this man would bow down till he got his head on the pavement and his movements were so extraordinary that all they could do was to look at him and watch him. The authorities did not know what to do with him. They could not say, 'You shall not be a Communicant', but they let him know indirectly that they thought his proceedings very ridiculous. 'Ah', said Sir Gilbert, 'you don't know all the little games that go on in Cathedrals.'[2]

There is no doubting Sir Gilbert's final reflection. Trollope's Barchester novels argue the case with regard to the clergy. Experience suggests that it is true of the behaviour of others too. Sometimes it will be 'men of the road', on other occasions eccentrics, and from time to time it may be psychopaths. Margaret remains a frequent visitor to one of our cathedrals. She brings her dog in with her and encourages him to sing;

she has had her previous four dogs stuffed and keeps them at home on her houseboat. Fred divides his day between the waiting room at the main railway station and the cathedral. Frequently he has conversations in the cathedral with the diocesan bishop; on one occasion, since the bishop made no attempt to reply, Fred threw a breakfast (bought for the bishop) at him. This needs to be put in the context of the fact that this particular diocesan bishop died in 1837.

Some of these unusual people come regularly to our cathedrals simply because they are places of shelter, refuge or sanctuary. But there is much more to it than that. There is about most cathedrals a very clear sense of *place*. At the most trivial level, this may simply relate to their being the local landmark: the tower, the spire or the lantern dominates the city and perhaps also the countryside for miles around. But there is more to it still. A cathedral is also seen as a place endowed with a particular aura of holiness. As others have written, it is 'sacred space'. This notion of being a notable sacred space has from earliest times marked off cathedrals from secular buildings, and even from other churches.

⟨∾⟩

The classic point of departure in marking off the particularity of a cathedral as a sacred space – or, more accurately, as a sacred *place* – is the association of the bishop with the building. Cathedrals are not simply large churches. There is admittedly much in common architecturally (and sometimes in feel) between English cathedrals and other great abbey or minster churches; but there is one crucial difference. A cathedral would not be a cathedral were it not for the presence in the building of the bishop's cathedra or chair. From the patristic period onward the cathedral was built with this in mind. The pattern out of which this grew was basilican: the Aula Palatina in Trier, a secular building, is a good example of this. Built by

Constantine the Great, it was used by the local Roman prefect, and consists of a rectangular building with an apsidal end. At the centre of the apse would have sat the prefect, surrounded by his college of advisers. This pattern was adopted by the Christian Church: Hagia Sophia in Constantinople still boasts an apse; the great basilican church of Santa Sabina on the Aventine Hill in Rome is similarly apsidally basilican in its structure. Some cathedrals have preserved this pattern: the Romanesque building in Norwich still contains the bishop's cathedra in its ancient position, high up in the eastern apse.

The position of the eastern cathedra in Norwich, elevated at the top of a flight of steps, focuses a further point about the essential nature of a cathedral. It is the *place* within which the teaching role of the bishop is concentrated. Traditionally, the cathedral was the auditorium within which the bishop gathered both clergy and people to expound to them the Christian faith; the tradition was handed on, on behalf of the Church, by the bishop in his cathedral. This practice has been rediscovered and revitalised in recent years by Carlo-Maria Martini, the cardinal archbishop of Milan: a formidable series of teaching seminars, lectures and courses has restored the great cathedral in Milan to its former role – a role which, in that place, reaches back to the time of St Ambrose in the late fourth century. It is a tradition that cathedrals and bishops can and ought to rediscover.

A PLACE OF DIVINE PRESENCE

The influence of the bishop in his cathedral, however, extends beyond teaching alone, in at least two other directions.

First, bishops built cathedrals to focus the presence of the divine. From earliest times this was inextricably bound into an understanding of a cathedral as a shrine. Where an episcopal basilica was established over the grave of a noted saint, the connection is obvious. The classic example is St Peter's, Rome:

the excavation of the site of the tomb of St Peter has helped to recapture a tradition that is now less immediate for many Christians. But this association with the saints was very powerful indeed during the period of the early Church. Peter Brown summarises this well. Reflecting on Hegel's discussion of piety and the holy in the medieval period, he writes:

> In the cult of the relics also, late-antique and early medi-aeval piety lived down with gusto to his [Hegel's] strictures. This cult gloried in particularity. *Hic locus est*: 'Here is the place', or simply *hic*, is a refrain that runs through the inscriptions on the early martyrs' shrines of North Africa. The holy was available in one *place* [my italics], and in each such place it was accessible to one group in a manner in which it could not be accessible to anyone situated elsewhere.[3]

It was a matter, then, as he puts it, of focusing the presence of God in a particular place. The significance of such a localised focus grew and became the centre of medieval pilgrimages: the shrines of St James at Compostela, St Boniface at Fulda and St Cuthbert at Durham are three classic examples. Numerous other places – some fairly obscure – could be quoted. In later medieval times this developed still further, the shrine of Thomas à Becket in Canterbury being perhaps the most celebrated case in England. Essential to the early development of this tradition, then, was the role of the bishop. Indeed, the prestige and power of the bishop might well be enhanced by such a development:

> Furthermore, building and ceremonial at such shrines would sum up more appositely than anywhere else the paradox of episcopal wealth . . . Such wealth and ceremonial would be deployed in the invisible presence of a figure who had taken on all the features of a later Roman *patronus*. The saint was the good *patronus*; he was the

patronus whose intercessions were successful, whose wealth was at the disposal of all, whose *potentia* was exercised without violence and to whom loyalty could be shown without constraint. The bishop could stand for him.[4]

The message is clear. The setting of the saint's shrine within the bishop's church brought together different focuses of the holy. Even where there is no shrine, relics could impart a sacred presence. In Norwich, beneath the ancient eastern bishop's throne is a reliquary niche. It reaches back to the beginnings of the cathedral and has always been a place of great holiness. From the ceiling of the niche emerges a flue which makes its way up to the floor beneath the bishop's feet. From the relic, God's Spirit is made present to each succeeding bishop in his ministry.

The establishment of this sacred building or sacred *place*, then, strengthens the office of bishop as a central focus within the wider community. This first happened in late Roman society, and it set in train a pattern of relationships which developed apace in medieval times. The bishop took on a prelatical and often princely presence, and established himself as a powerful focus in the secular as well as the sacred community. Happily much of that pattern of prelacy has now disappeared, and thankfully the Church now rarely exercises temporal power. Nevertheless, the legend survives. As the traveller enters County Durham, even the motorway signs announce: 'You are now entering the land of the Prince Bishops'. More significantly, the expectations placed upon bishops and their cathedrals in relation to the city and the region has remained. In England, the cathedral is often both the 'civic church' and also the focus of religious references for the county. It is such because it is the *'place* of the bishop'.

THE PLACE OF THE BISHOP

The second direction of episcopal influence in cathedrals is effectively ecclesiological. The cathedral is an ecclesiological focus, because the bishop himself is the focus of unity for the Church in that county, region and diocese. While the Church of God remains divided, the truth of this phrase, 'focus of unity', is obviously compromised. Nevertheless it is upon this notion of episcopacy that most theological dialogue aimed at visible unity has been based. It is on the office of bishop that unity should centre; the bishop's ministry is one of those aspects of the life of the Church that holds Christians together in communion with each other in one place. Hence the presence of two bishops in one locality emphasises the damaging disunity which still persists.

In being the focus of unity for a particular locality, however, the bishop also makes possible the links of the local church with the universal. During sub-apostolic times, neither the theological *raison d'être* nor the functions of priest and bishop were clearly differentiated. It was only as the Church developed thereafter that the need arose for a wider conspectus for oversight. It was at this point that the need for a clear focus of unity in a particular place became essential. The episcopate came to fulfil this function, with priests acting as focuses within smaller eucharistic communities; the Eucharist within which they presided was still the bishop's Eucharist – that is, it still associated itself with the universal Church through the wider ministry of the bishop. The bishop was also part of a wider college of episcopal oversight – a college that assumed the role of handing on the teaching of the 'Catholic Church'. This is clearly seen early on at the Council of Nicaea in 325. This Council marked the beginning of the Church's efforts to clarify its corporate belief about the nature of Christ and his part in the economy of salvation. We can see how the teaching role of the bishop, which we have already mentioned in relation to the place of cathedrals, relates to the episcopal task of focusing communion in the universal Church. This pattern has been reflected in ecumenical dialogue. In *Baptism, Eucharist and Ministry*, a document reflecting the views of a very wide range of theologians across the Churches, the universal significance of the bishop's role is emphasised. Collegiality with other orders of ministry is mentioned there too:

> [Bishops] relate the Christian community in their area to the wider Church, and the universal Church to their community. They, in communion with the presbyters and deacons and the whole community, are responsible for the orderly transfer of ministerial authority in the Church.[6]

This pattern of collegiality and universality means that cathedrals themselves become signs of the wider Church, as they reflect the ministry of their bishops. One of the essential roles of cathedrals continues to be their ministry within a diocese, reminding all within a diocese that they are part of a wider community of Christians throughout the world. The variety of diocesan services and events which takes place in cathedrals reflects this role. But within the Church of England, membership of a province and of the Anglican Communion is also reflected through the witness of the cathedrals. In the work of the Anglican–Roman Catholic International Commission, and through the visits of successive archbishops of Canterbury to Rome, a still wider collegiality has been identified. Archbishop Runcie, on his visit to Pope John Paul II in 1989, said: 'Could not all Christians come to reconsider the kind of primacy the bishop of Rome exercised within the early Church, a "presiding in love" for the sake of the unity of the Churches in the diversity of their mission?'[7]

More recently still, Pope John Paul has asked other Christians if they would be prepared to assist him in defining the role of the bishop of Rome in the sort of terms set out above.[8] Each of these moves aims to repair the brokenness of the

Church by restoring clearer links between the universal and the local. None of this can have any reality without the symbolic presence of bishops in each locality. That presence is made visible through the existence of cathedrals.

The presence and role of bishops, then, is essential in any theological understanding of cathedrals. This is the more obvious when we view a cathedral in its sacramental role. On Maundy Thursday, the diocesan bishop gathers together his clergy for the blessing of the oils. Often this is accompanied by the clergy reaffirming their episcopal, priestly and diaconal vows. At Easter, the ancient custom of the bishop baptising and confirming in his cathedral at the time of the paschal celebrations is beginning to be recovered. The bishop also frequently celebrates the Eucharist in his cathedral at the great feasts of Easter, Christmas and Pentecost. This celebration of the great sacraments of salvation means that cathedrals proclaim the Christian message of redemption, and so have a prophetic role within contemporary society; indeed, this same proclamation of the sacraments of salvation happens continuously through the daily and weekly ministry of the cathedral. Cathedrals remain then the *places, par excellence*, of the Christian sacraments; their presence proclaims the drama of salvation. A subtle irony is implied: theologically cathedrals are both symbols of the universality of the Christian Church and the Gospel it proclaims, and also of the particularity of the message of salvation proclaimed by word and sacrament.

༺❦༻

A PLACE FOR PUBLIC DAILY PRAYER

We have already begun to appreciate the significance of liturgy and worship in the life of cathedrals. Alongside the sacramental focus there has also been, from earliest times, an ancient tradition of daily prayer and the saying of the office. A cathedral is thus also a *place* that honours the rhythm of each day in a sustained pattern of prayer. One of the main roots of the daily office stems from the so-called cathedral office – thus described to distinguish it from the daily hours of prayer honoured in the monasteries. The key factor about the cathedral office was its public nature. Instead of resonating with the monastic patterns of seven hours of prayer, cathedrals resonated with the natural rhythms of daybreak and dusk. From the beginning, the public office in cathedrals took advantage of the fact that they were large city churches. They offered music, drama and the participation of the people. One of the key factors was that, in the early tradition of the cathedral office, there were no books; instead the people were encouraged to participate with the use of repeated antiphons, responses and refrains.

It is true that the public office was not the sole preserve of cathedrals for very long. Nevertheless this was where it began, and this gave to the cathedrals a role that has never been totally lost. In the East, the cathedral was effectively the secular church. The catechumens (trainee Christians) were present during the office (so it was seen to include a teaching element), and it was celebrated by the whole community.[9] In the West, the Ambrosian pattern in Milan offers us a classic example: the psalms were central, and the mixture of canticles, antiphons and scriptural readings was there. In the West, the cathedral and the monastic origins of the office were blurred from early on. In both East and West, however, the cathedral tradition recognised the natural rhythms of the day, celebrating the rising sun and then the evening light with the lighting of the candle or *lucernarium*.[10]

At the heart of public prayer in the cathedrals lay the recitation of the daily office, entirely from memory and so without the use of books. The introduction of breviaries into the life of the medieval Church, in the mid thirteenth century, both for individual and corporate use, marked the beginning of the privatisation of the daily office. In itself the evolution of breviaries was inevitable; it made the content of the office more easily accessible and not simply the possession of the *cognoscenti*. That said, it took the medieval Church further down the road towards private and individualised devotion which also made its way into the celebration of the Mass. The corporate and the public are not themselves inextricably linked, but the corporate tradition in daily prayer certainly supported the public nature of the office. It was the cathedrals that preserved this practice for the longest period of time. George Guiver notes:

> At Lincoln in the fifteenth century no one was allowed in choir with a book, save for the dean, precentor, chancellor and treasurer. In France, the Council of Narbonne in 1551 forbade the canons to have any book in choir with them, even a personal breviary.[11]

Prayer was thus rooted in the sacred space of the cathedral, rather than in the proliferation of books which so easily diverted the impulse into the private spiritual lives of each individual. In the Eastern Church, something of this same pattern is still traceable in the corporate singing of countless litanies in Orthodox Vespers.

Interestingly enough it was effectively the cathedral model that Cranmer revived in his transformation of the office into the twice-daily pattern of Morning and Evening Prayer. By then it was overlain with the Reformation preoccupations of making Scripture accessible and translating the liturgy into the vernacular; all this was included in the single volume, *Book of the Common Prayer and Administration of the Sacraments* of 1549, that is the first prayer book of King Edward VI. Nevertheless the pattern which issued from Cranmer's revision was exactly that of honouring the opening and the closing of the day with a daily rhythm of prayer. The collects of Matins and Evensong set the scene precisely: 'O Lord our heavenly Father, almighty and ever-living God, which has safely brought us to the beginning of this day'; and 'Lighten our darkness, we beseech thee, O Lord, and by thy great mercy defend us from all perils and dangers of this night'. Although admittedly Cranmer had culled the material for his new offices from the monastic hours, it was the cathedral pattern that was to emerge. Furthermore, Cranmer's aim had been precisely to restore the public recitation of the office and to encourage the laity to join the minister in this pattern of daily prayer.

His intention had also been to pen out a rhythm of prayer to which all the people might resonate, not only in cathedrals, but in every parish church in the land. Indeed, it remains the canonical requirement upon all Church of England priests that they should say the office daily. References to the 'whole congregation' in the Book of Common Prayer make it clear that others were intended to join the minister. In the event, through a process of historical development, it has been the cathedrals that have come closest to Cranmer's ideal – due both to the expectations placed upon them and the resources available to them. In every English cathedral the evening office will be *sung* at least once (in almost every case more than once) per week. Both Morning and Evening Prayer are said daily and publicly. Often a sprinkling of devout lay people and occasional visitors will join the clergy.

With the development of a rich and sophisticated musical repertoire, English cathedrals have further returned to one of those central functions for which they existed from earliest times – that is, the public recitation of the daily office. Sung Evensong has become part of English culture. But the significance of the public singing of the office is far deeper than simply being a regularised ecclesiastical concert performance. The office performed in this way remains a public profession of the faith, a recitation of the story which stands at the heart of the Christian faith. Furthermore it picks up another important theological strand: sung cathedral Evensong includes an element that is deliberately non-participatory for many of those who attend. The congregation for much of the time does not perform, but is done to. The office is not said so as to win us grace; instead, that grace is received simply by being present. This pattern is established at the heart of the gospel story: on the night before his passion Jesus hands himself over – not to do, but to offer himself into the will of others. Even ministers in Evensong often find themselves being ministered to rather than ministering. By this process of passive participation, no one is excluded. Books are almost unnecessary – we are not far from the earliest principles of the cathedral office. Cathedrals are *places* where prayer is publicly offered. They are signs of the universality of the Christian Gospel, and minister universally to all humanity. At their most effective they are in sharp contrast to churches which deliberately gather to themselves an eclectic congregation.

From early times, then, the theological rationale which has underpinned cathedrals has brought together a mixture of the incarnational and redemptive aspects of the Christian Gospel. In their regular performance of the great sacraments, they have proclaimed to the world the saving grace of the one who, in giving himself, offered resurrection and new life to all humanity. In Johannine language: 'I, when I am lifted up from the earth, will draw all men to myself', and from the same chapter, 'Unless a grain of wheat falls into the earth and dies, it remains alone: but if it dies, it bears much fruit' (John 12: 32,24). At the same time, the universality of God's grace through Christ's incarnation has been proclaimed by the presence of the bishop's chair at the heart of a cathedral, and by the public recitation of the divine office. Each of these is offered to a wider world so that a cathedral may become a focus which draws 'all sorts and conditions of people'. To use a term coined by Reinhold Niebuhr, cathedrals have been both channels of and recognisers of 'common grace'. Common grace is that means by which God's presence is made plain through the institutions within society.

✎

A PLACE TO FOCUS DIVINE REDEMPTION

The strength, beauty and implicit triumphalism of cathedrals hardly make them the most obvious channels of redemptive grace. They appear to speak of a Constantinian model of the Church more suitably mirrored in purely incarnational theology. Interestingly enough, however, cathedrals frequently point powerfully to redemption. In Canterbury, the site of Thomas à Becket's martyrdom and the modern Chapel of Twentieth-Century Martyrs both remind us of humanity's fallenness and longing for salvation. The Abbey Church at St Alban's stands on the site of the tomb of the earliest known Christian martyr in Britain. The shrine of St Alban was recently restored to remind us to honour this early martyr, predating by some 400 years the Columban and Augustinian missions of the early seventh century. A number of other cathedrals have chapels dedicated to the Holy Innocents or to those who have been martyred for their faith.

Ministry to the disadvantaged and the perplexed has become a practical means by which cathedrals witness to this redemption. Those ministered to comprise a very mixed group. They include the lost and the troubled, the weary and the sad, and that most elusive group of all – seekers after faith. There can hardly be a cathedral that does not gather to itself a small group of people who have become disconnected from the mainstream of contemporary society. We return to the characters with whom we began. There is Fred, who was cashiered from the army because of his drinking habits. After living in a tent for some years, he now has a place at the night shelter – but the cathedral is his home for most of the day. There is Margaret, a grandish lady who suffered a total nervous breakdown and now lives on a houseboat with her taxidermised pets of the past 20 years; she has another cathedral as her regular home. With the demise of much institutionalised psychiatric care, larger numbers of those who cannot cope come daily to our cathedrals for comfort and companionship. The seekers may come from far and wide. They may be bereaved, they may simply have been searching for meaning throughout their entire lives. They warm to cathedrals, for they know that they are somehow holy. They would applaud the sentiments of Bruckner's *'Locus Iste'*, without being able quite to explain why. But they appreciate cathedrals too because in those vast acres of semi-contained space, distant Romanesque vistas, and myriad Gothic arcades, they may walk unhindered and allow their thoughts to crystallise. One such person wrote recently to a dean:

> I cannot adequately express my heartfelt thanks to your cathedral. Some seven years ago I wandered through it with a heavy heart seeking solace. I had never been a believer but I was a troubled soul. I had walked through one church after another. On this day I had the courage to approach one of the clergy who listened sensitively and offered some reflections. That was the beginning of my journey home to God.

Cathedrals thus reflect a mixed theological economy.

This mixed theological economy is a torch that has been passed on to the present generation as we reflect upon the theological rationale of cathedrals and their ministry. The rehearsing of salvation history through the performance of the great sacraments has recaptured a place more central to the life of English cathedrals than perhaps at any time since the Reformation. The Easter vigil at Portsmouth, combining a great Eucharist with the bishop presiding at the sacraments of baptism and confirmation, stands in direct continuity with the patterns of the early Church. Regular diocesan confirmations in Norwich, which take people in pilgrimage through the building and which remind them of the passion, death and resurrection of Christ, re-present the story of redemption. The daily offering of the Eucharist, and the increasing centrality of the Eucharist in diocesan and other celebrations in all our cathedrals, further press home this point.

But the redemptive strand within Christian worship has been emphasised in contemporary times by more than the sacraments alone. The regular youth gatherings on Easter Monday in Guildford, St Albans and Canterbury proclaim the passion and its sequel to a new generation. Often these reinforce the cathedral as 'the place' of proclamation by using a large, stark cross, sometimes outside the building, around which the young people gather. In Salisbury the performance of the Way of the Cross through the streets of the city, culminating in the celebration of resurrection within the cathedral, uses street theatre to good effect. Both the sacramental and non-sacramental point to an *explicit* theology defining the nature of cathedrals as 'sacred places'. The presence of the bishop focuses this explicit theological strand.

PLACE – IMPLICIT AND EXPLICIT THEOLOGY

As the pages of this book have indicated, cathedrals draw to themselves an extraordinary spectrum of different people; they have remained 'common ground'.[12] The tradition of the nave of a medieval cathedral being the 'people's church' has lived on – and to a large extent this understanding has been applied to the whole building. The variety of different motives which prompt people to visit cathedrals today is enormous. In Durham, Canterbury, Worcester, St Albans, Chichester and Lincoln there remain either the shrines or the sites of shrines of local saints. Cuthbert's tomb behind the high altar in Durham remains magnetic in its attraction to pilgrims; it is complemented by the tomb of Bede in the Galilee Chapel. The pavement before the shrine of St Hugh of Lincoln has been hollowed out through the constant kneeling of devout pilgrims at the shrine. Pilgrimage remains an essential strand within ascetic theology, and in an age of nostalgia is increasingly attractive to a puzzled but still interested wider non-Christian world.[13]

Not all, then, will immediately recognise cathedrals as *places* of bishops or of the Christian sacraments. How precisely will they interpret these great, mysterious, but sometimes daunting and overwhelming buildings? Will they recognise the altar as the focus of the Eucharist, that which identifies the Christian Church? Will they know that the font is the place of baptism, where new Christians are taken down into the grave with Christ, there to be raised with him? Certainly each expects something of these great buildings – but it is often an expectation so inchoate as to be virtually untraceable clearly upon the screen of human experience. Underpinning this expectation is the belief that these are *places* where at the very least there is a sense of 'presence'. It may be nothing more than the presence of a historical context out of which the cathedral grew. It may be an overpowering sense of the numinous, or a compelling conviction that the world is a world of purpose and not meaninglessness and that there is a presence which convinces us of the truth of this experience. The one thing which subtly links together each of these different expectations is linked to an *implicit* theology. It is not about the direct proclamation of the word of God; it is not even the logic behind a finely performed sacramental enactment of the Christian drama of salvation.

Instead, this implicit theological strand points to the grace of God working through humanity in often intricate, subtle and elusive ways. To recall Niebuhr's term, it is another example of 'common grace'. It is, however, common, and not cheap, grace; it may indeed be costly for the individual and equally costly to the institution. If cathedrals are effectively to minister to all these different sorts and conditions of humanity, then an awareness of the varied needs, hopes and expectations of all of these people is essential. Having thus become aware, the great host of volunteers and paid staff that make cathedral life possible must then reflect upon how to be effective channels of this common grace. The great variety, elusiveness and random-ness of such experience does not undermine the need for training our paid staff and volunteers. Nor indeed does it remove the need for us to interpret these buildings in an age where cathedrals may seem to some increasingly anachronistic.

'Mad people', Sir Gilbert said, 'come to cathedrals.' It has always been notoriously difficult to define how to judge madness. What are the criteria for sanity? Whatever basis we might choose to use, it is inconceivable that the cavalcade of people who visit our cathedrals would not be well represented – and that is true whether we begin our definition from the point of view of sanity or madness. The *implicit* and the *explicit* theologies underpinning cathedrals as *places* which focus the presence of God require theologians to take seriously both the incarnational and redemptive strands within Christian theology. A greater awareness of the implicit and explicit, the incarnational and redemptive, may make us more sensitive to these extraordinary *places* which have channelled God's grace to countless generations.

NINE

HUMAN EBB AND FLOW

Cathedrals and people

CHRISTOPHER LEWIS

A bishop recently urged a very beautiful cathedral to break out of its 'paradisal prison' in order that it might use its strength for serving, not being served.[1] 'Paradisal prison': the expression is helpful discovering how cathedrals handle the hopes and expectations of those who feel drawn to them. For 'paradise' and 'prison' point to a basic paradox. Here are lovely, great buildings, aiming to be signs of the very gates of heaven – and yet they are human creations and they gather to themselves much that repels. They are focal points for love and hate, around which have eddied all kinds of sinful and holy activity. For some people, they appear as symbols of oppression and power, or as an endless drain on resources both human and financial: in the twelfth century, St Bernard railed against the foolish extravagance of cathedral building.[2] For others, they are holy places, of inexpressible spiritual significance. Those who live alongside them, sometimes it seems almost under them, may know both sides of the paradox. If those who govern them have a distinguishing fault, it is complacency, sheltering under the frequently repeated mantra, 'for the glory of God'.

Books and articles on cathedrals often agonise over their

purpose, exploring their function and usefulness – a modern fascination. Are they for worship and mission, for theological study, for the bishop to teach in? Perhaps they and their communities are for all these purposes and more – but what *are* they and for whom? That is what F. S. M. Bennett set out to examine in his book, *The Nature of a Cathedral*, published in 1925 when he was dean of Chester. He saw himself as uncovering the original nature of cathedrals, enabling them to be accessible. He observed:

> It is hardly to be wondered at that what began as a Family House of Prayer for all, has come to be regarded as something very like the special property of a small corporation, that it does not strike people as outrageous if the said small corporation charges those to whom the cathedral really belongs, sixpence or a shilling for going round what is theirs or, more monstrous still, excludes them from it altogether on Sundays between the services.[3]

It is not clear when Bennett thought that cathedrals 'began', but his intention is nevertheless plain: to return the buildings to their rightful owners from whom they had been removed – much in the way that eighteenth-century landlords enclosed common land. So he commended an 'aggressive hospitableness', over against the usual stiffness, in order to return the cathedral to the people.

Significantly, Bennett did not wish to reclaim cathedrals for tourists. He wanted the cathedral really to belong to the people of the diocese in which it is set. They were the true owners, not the proprietorial clergy and not the city, for the cathedral 'will always be tempted to become too parochial in its city and its city will always love to have it so'.

⁓

Yet it is with the clergy that it is appropriate to start. In

1777 the parish of Aylsham, a pleasant Norfolk market town, received a new vicar after due decision by the patron of the parish, the dean and chapter of Canterbury Cathedral. History does not relate whether he was a good vicar, only that he dined now and again with a neighbour, the diarist James Woodforde, and drank spruce beer. The circumstances of his appointment are, however, recorded in the reminiscences of the Revd George Gilbert who relates that a Canterbury Cathedral statute required those entering for a service to bow towards the dean's stall when he was occupying it:

> In obedience to this Statute the clergy moving towards the altar etc. always have bowed towards the Dean's stall. There was a Minor Canon (named Taswell) who disliked this and refused to observe the rule. Whereupon he was threatened with deprivation. So being obliged to conform he always bowed down to the ground in a very ridiculous manner, and whenever he met the Dean or a Canon in the street, he did the same, saying 'good day my worthy master'. The chapter finding him (as a wag) very trouble-some, gave him the good living of Aylsham in Norfolk, and thus were quit of him. After he had accepted the living and before he left Canterbury, he met Miss Hester Gosling, one of that clever Mint Yard family, on her way to Service. 'What going to the Puppet Shew, Miss Hester?' said he. 'No Sir' replied Miss Gosling, 'that Exhibition has ceased. Punch is ordered into Norfolk.'[4]

Cathedrals are fascinating not only to visiting clergy like Gilbert, but also to novelists and, of course, to those of the inner circle themselves. The media must now be added to the list of those peering over the precinct wall. Whether the goings-on inside are in fact odder than those of, say, a hospital, a factory or a university college, is debatable. But perhaps the stories 'stick' in a way that they would not do elsewhere because they are told in the context of a large and durable building. They may also attract because of the enjoyable chasm between eternal aspirations and human buffoonery. When a recent dean of Lincoln retired he told of an Easter service in the cathedral:

> The choir was packed; so packed indeed that some ladies, finding nowhere else for them to go after the procession, settled in one or other of the 53 Canons' stalls – and, despite the fact that there was nowhere else for them to sit, were being vigorously winkled out by the Vergers and left to stand like a huddle of over-shepherded sheep in the centre of the floor. Bishop Kenneth Riches said to me afterwards that he would never come to the Cathedral again. The Chapter said that the Canons had a right to protect their stalls from misuse and I wrote some 50 letters to the Canons asking them to allow women in their stalls, which they did.[5]

The clergy behave in a way which is conditioned (although not, of course, determined) by their context. The Christian faith is a broad and many-faceted collection of beliefs and practices, so people are inevitably selective within it, according to the circumstances in which they find themselves. The group of clergy assembled around a cathedral will tend to behave in a way which is consistent with the building and its traditions; in that sense, the building 'wins', for it is a magnetic master or mistress which was there long before them and will be there long after them. They have a job to do which seems to be that of serving the interests of the building and institution, and developing its strengths. Although in constant need of repair, the cathedral is as near to being eternal as any man-made object. It does not doubt or ask questions; it dictates the answers to them.

The clergy are thus set in a context which influences them powerfully, often both living and working in close proximity to each other (in a way which very few other people do), and on a task which throws them together, while relating them to an emotionally charged and physically restricted building. They may be selected (by different agencies) not so much because they are team players, but for particular talents which they are supposed to possess.

Factors such as these may result in cheerful anecdotes of eccentricity – but may also lead to what Archbishop Lang referred to as 'the cathedral blight', of which there are examples both throughout cathedrals' history and today. The blight does not only affect clergy, although they may catch it more severely than others. Paid staff may be similarly blighted, as may some laity who become so bound up with the supposed importance of the institution that they behave in a pugnacious and proprietorial manner. Musicians, administrators and stalwart volunteers may come to see the cathedral as being in business for their own benefit. That is not to say that blight is inevitable, or that it is caught in any more than a minority of cases. It is important, however, in a book on cathedrals, to recognise the danger and to ask whether there are measures which can assist cathedrals in having co-operative teams of clergy and lay people bent on tasks of use to the Church as a whole.

The first such measure is to return to F. S. M. Bennett and to recognise that there are many who have a share in cathedrals and that 'the small corporation' of the clergy and their immediate entourage needs to be supplemented and checked upon. The 'corporation' is often defended as being monastic (living, praying and working together) – but that argument omits reference to the monastic rule, structure and discipline which are now lacking. From the very beginning of cathedrals in their post-Reformation form, this kind of point was made: Thomas Cranmer saw nothing but trouble coming from having what he called a 'sect of prebendaries' gathered around a cathedral with, in his view, rather too little to do.[6] He wanted the money available to be used to pay teachers instead, for he saw a canon becoming 'neither a learner, nor a teacher, but a good viander'; others have thought likewise.

Cathedral clergy are now busier, perhaps at times too busy – but they should not have a monopoly of control of cathedrals. It is not in doubt that they should pray and work together, at least for some of the time; but when it comes to the government of cathedrals, others have an interest and a part to play. Cathedrals are too important to be left in the hands of one category of stakeholder alone.

Cathedrals are, secondly, places which thrive on being served by clergy with diverse commitments which they pursue from, and bring back to, the cathedral; in that way, not all the attention is taken up with the building and its immediate concerns. And thirdly, it is not desirable that clergy should have permanent tenure, for otherwise mistakes cannot be rectified and new life cannot be given to the team, other than on retirement or death!

The evidence from history and contemporary practice seems to support the theory that cathedrals have a restricting effect on those who never move from them, and a liberating effect on those who visit them only occasionally.[7] The pilgrim is in a better position than the dean, for the former returns home renewed by a spiritual experience. In Durham or St Albans, as in Jerusalem, little good stems from hovering over a shrine and losing interest in everything else. Theologically, that is not incarnation but spiritual stagnation. So the clergy may learn from the other groups who believe that they 'own' cathedrals – and indeed, they should find ways in which these others can contribute to the life of these pieces of common ground. The most prominent new constituency is the visitor.

‿❧‿

Tourism is a comparatively recent phenomenon. It is an activity which thrives when there is peace and which is dependent on prosperity and mobility. In time of war or of economic disaster, recreational travel ceases almost immediately, and those places which have depended on it lose their livelihood. So it is an unreliable activity in which to invest too heavily. But the temptation to do so is almost irresistible, because tourism brings such immediate economic returns. It may spell confusion for the tourist, entail demeaning jobs for many workers and induce a shift of resources into ephemeral activities, but overall the hosts seem to see it as beneficial.

How should cathedrals react? Most have welcomed tourists with open arms; they have instituted a 'ministry of welcome'. Here is a source of finance and a justification for existence, with impressive visitor-figures to quote. And perhaps the people who come may be seen as the equivalent of the pilgrims of the past. They may ask questions such as, 'Where are the dungeons?' or, 'Are you open on Christmas day?', which show that they are not very clear about where they are – but could it still be that tourists are really earnest seekers after truth? Much in the same way that churches give the benefit of the doubt to those seeking baptism, cathedrals welcome visitors and alter facilities accordingly.

Even more significant for cathedrals than a tourist boom is the fact that people in developed countries have not only become geographical tourists but also historical ones. Past times have become something which people tour, much as they tour foreign parts. They are in search of new experiences in quaint places, and 'the past is a foreign country, they do things differently there'.[8] The effect of this phenomenon is that visitors are often concerned to explore 'heritage' and, rather than immersing themselves in the past, take what looks desirable from history, much as they would select geographical areas as pleasurable for a holiday. For many, the past is not something which challenges or repels: it is preserved with care and used to meet present needs. Inspiration has been replaced by conservation. What was history is altered in order to make it a marketable and tourable commodity.

The result of these developments is that cathedrals may be seen as part of a gutted and preserved heritage, somewhat in the manner of George Washington's false teeth, carefully displayed in the Smithsonian Institution. Here are relics, time machines, theme parks, domesticated in order to satisfy the time-tourist. The past is made palatable by interpretation, and where there is an interpretative centre, many do not bother to see the object itself, for the interpretation is more readily digestible. True history may be tedious: 'You can't re-enact a siege. Everybody would get bored and go home.'⁹ So the time-tourist selects and conflates; hence the visitor to Canterbury who entered with the question: 'Where was this guy Becket shot?'

There is no doubt that tourists are now among those with a part to play in cathedrals. Cathedrals have been happy to be treated as a sector of the nation's heritage and to respond in much the same way as other visitor-attractions. They talk of controlling visitor-flow and may consider charges for entry. They lay on guided tours which concentrate on history and architecture, and they may build an interpretative centre for visitors from which people emerge from their experience of the past through the inevitable shop.

There is an extent to which cathedrals cannot avoid these developments – and nor would it be desirable for them to do so. It is essential to their missionary task that they stay open to all. Many of them are old buildings, and they are churches of a religion which is inescapably historical. Yet the fact that Christianity is a historical religion means that it should have the experience to handle new attitudes to history, rather than just responding blindly to them. Christian faith looks to the Jesus of history and to the seminal documents of the Bible, but it does not separate that Jesus from the Christ of faith and, whatever the perceptions of the heritage industry, the prime emphasis of the Church is, or should be, on the present and the future. In a cyclical liturgical understanding of history, what was past is appropriated and made present, so that it is significant for Christian life in the present and the future.

The question, then, becomes: how are cathedrals best used for Christian purposes, given the new fact of streams of visitors? In order to answer that question, one kind of visitor not yet mentioned needs to be considered: 'odd' people. The presence of odd people in cathedrals, in quite large numbers, may be explained by many factors: they may be more open to God than the apparently less odd; they may sense that cathedrals are safe places where admission is usually free; they may know that there are people in the building who are liable to respond in a more friendly manner than elsewhere. Whatever the explanation, there are strong reasons within the Christian tradition for making the way in which we respond to those on the margins of society a test case. The marginal (and the less marginal) respond to a holy place, a welcoming atmosphere, activity and human contact. They are happy to be around in a place where people are doing normal religious things: praying, writing prayers, lighting candles, worshipping, gazing at the cross. They remark on the fact that the significance of the place is clearer when the organ is being played or when there is incense in the air; they are far less concerned to find the shiny excellence for which cathedrals are sometimes commended, and they certainly do not wish to be processed through a lot of interpretation. For them, the best interpretative centre of all is the cathedral building itself, in use for Christian purposes. Holiness has more to do with live people than with dead ones. Much of what is true for those whom we label 'odd' is true for all.

There are all kinds of pressures on cathedrals to assimilate themselves to the tourist and heritage industries. They should respond reflectively, and so cater for visitors hospitably while retaining their central purpose as Christian churches. They will need consciously to resist merely being seen as heritage trails; little historical information has to be displayed, there being much significance in actual activity and in some pointers to the religious importance of a font or of a chapel dedicated to modern martyrs. The visitor is then taken seriously and responded to, but in a way which maintains the integrity of the place.

~&~

It is through the life of the congregation that the place keeps its essential character as a church. Cathedral clergy have an ambivalent attitude to 'their' congregations. It is often said that the members are unusual in that cathedral congregations prefer quiet anonymity in contrast to the convivial collectiveness of some parishes, or that they are really music lovers who have little interest in other aspects of the Christian faith. Such generalisations may be used to justify a lack of normal congregational activity or a failure to consult the congregation on matters of importance in cathedral life. And yet the clergy are dependent on them, Sunday by Sunday, for being the core of the worshippers. In fact, cathedral congregations are not very different from others in their character; they should be set apart by being more outward-looking than other congregations, because it is impressed on them at every turn that there are many other people who have an interest in the cathedral and a right to use it.

At a time when religious practice is less prevalent than it was in the last century, the trend has been for many church congregations to become smaller, more highly committed and therefore more difficult to enter. For the members, the sense is of a gathered group of people who show their Christian love for one another; but newcomers or strangers may experience a closed circle facing inwards, backs to the world. Whatever else cathedrals suffer from, it is hard for that to happen, for it is in the nature of the place for there to be ebb and flow.

Among those who come and go are members of other churches. Church of England cathedrals are both the most Anglican of places, with their choral Evensongs and their bishops, and yet also the least Anglican, for they potentially belong to all. That fact opens them up to be places of ecumenical activity and experiment: safe places where unity can be worked at. What might seem threatening or illegal in a church congregation can be contained within a cathedral, and what is learned is then passed on to others. Cathedrals have great and unrealised ecumenical potential.

It is the congregational members (of all churches) who not only give life to a cathedral, but also provide many of the large team of volunteers needed to keep the place in being. If guides are to be weaned from offering mere heritage tours, it is the congregation who can best help them, for its members can speak from experience of Christian faith and mission.

⤳⤶⤳

Beyond regular worshippers and volunteers is another group – namely the diocese and, in particular, the bishop. It is the bishop's symbolic presence, in the form of the throne, which makes a cathedral a cathedral, and in this place the bishop himself may preach, teach and arrange large diocesan occasions. Bishop and cathedral are the two main ways in which the diversity of a diocese is given a visible focus; in an episcopal Church, the two must be closely related, and where that relationship breaks down, the consequences are unhappy for all. In 1328 Archbishop Melton of York was prevented by force from holding a visitation or inspection of 'his' cathedral, and there have been similar occasions of antipathy down the centuries. Yet the Anglican tradition of preserving some separation ensures that the cathedral has a life of its own and does not become wholly drawn into diocesan affairs. The cathedral may also protect the bishop from the demands of the diocese by providing a place where he especially belongs, and where other interests and perspectives (civic, international) are given prominence. The bishop has a main place to which to belong, and the cathedral in its turn has a representative link with the diocese of which it is part.

The way in which the link with the diocese is actually expressed on a daily basis is a delicate matter for which both cathedral and diocese have responsibility. To use F. S. M. Bennett's term, an 'aggressive hospitableness' is necessary, for otherwise the cathedral, as a comparatively large institution, will inevitably attract accusations of superiority and distance. A somewhat earlier student of cathedrals, E. W. Benson, wrote of the need for a diocese and its clergy to have 'great bright, central houses of work, worship, counsel and sympathy'.[10] Occasions need to be created when people from the diocese come to what is their own, enjoy it and perhaps experience the Church as something which is much wider than the congregation. The ideal is for there to be two-way traffic between cathedral and diocese, with cathedral resources used for the benefit of all, and with members of churches in the diocese showing commitment to their cathedral.

This consciousness of belonging to the diocese is of crucial importance in rooting the cathedral in the life of the Church. Cathedrals, as this essay tries to demonstrate, have many groups concerned with them, and it is easy for them to listen only to the most congenial. If a diocese is making what seem to be excessive demands, is there not some national or congregational role which takes precedence? Cathedral authorities may also be encouraged to dilute their relationship with the diocese by the tendency for cathedrals as a group to refer increasingly to each other. As outside aid and conservation agencies treat cathedrals as a category distinct from others, so that becomes their self-perception: they may see themselves as a Church within a Church, with its own special theology and task. The frequent meetings between employees of different cathedrals are one sign of this danger. Yet for reasons central to its theological rationale, the cathedral cannot extract itself from bishop and diocese. It has a duty to the place where it is.

✎∽✐

The cathedral is also in a city. Bennett saw the cathedral city as a rival to the diocese, being eager to take over the time and energies of the cathedral. To the city could be added the county or counties – but not as rivals, more as further groups and individuals who look to the cathedral in some way. Reference has already been made to the consequences in religious practice of an apparently more secular society. Churches are perceived as belonging increasingly to the explicitly committed. Somewhere, the links need to be kept open with those who have a sense that religion does not just belong to the religious. In cathedrals, *par excellence*, religious symbols and activity are public rather than privatised property. Here voluntary organisations may come to offer to God what they are doing, and to be affirmed in their work. The lord lieutenant and the high sheriff will come for county occasions such as the justices service. The mayor, whether a Christian or not, may want an annual civic service when representatives of the community can be together as at no other time. Schools come for annual dedications and carol services.

Cathedrals belong to their cities, and those who say that cathedral cities have a special atmosphere are not just being romantic. Cities sprawl and grow and they often do not have natural boundaries; all the more, they need a centre and focal point around which much life revolves, even if many of the citizens never or rarely enter it. Here is a building which may bring a sense of pride and beauty, even a certain eerie power, and may also be some sign of the interweaving of the temporal and the eternal; over against fragmentation, the cathedral may stand for order and integration. What is more, it is large and durable enough to take risks and be known for adventure and experiment, much of which may spring from the city surrounding it: inter-faith festivals, happenings for young people, prophetic work for justice and peace. Events which might not otherwise be particularly significant become special because of the building in which they take place.

~~~

There are many other groups which have an interest. On common ground, grazing rights are difficult to define and it is undesirable that they should be too tightly controlled. There is no such thing as a trespasser. In one place, it may be the Royal Navy that sees the cathedral as its own; in another, an international network of those working for reconciliation; in another, something as extensive and difficult to define as the Anglican Communion. Yet the central purpose of a cathedral as a Christian church has to be affirmed; concert-goers need to realise that it is not a concert hall; conservationists, that it must develop and live; donors, that they are not shareholders; those in search of peace, that it will be noisy; those who see it as a market-place, that it needs its times and places of quiet.

Cathedrals are nothing if they are not accessible holy places in which all kinds of people feel that they belong. They should be alive, like an animal – and not a domestic one. Their 'ownership' should be vigorously protected as being definitely and in principle uncertain. It is tempting for cathedrals to use their power over people in order only to associate with the most biddable or exalted, and thus to avoid collisions between different groups. But to succumb to that temptation is to lose their central role. If those with an interest are not allowed their stake, then the few people who hover over the building, with power, become obsessive and their fantasies multiply. The best cure is the many other people, with their contrasting perspectives. For here all sorts come for solace and renewal, and from here they go out, it is hoped, with new insight. It is inevitable that different groups will try to possess cathedrals and call them their own, perhaps charging 'visitors' to enter, or in some other way putting up barriers against those who wish to be in them or to pass through them. In one place it may be the clergy who are possessive; in another, the regular congregation; in another, the city; in another, the tourist industry; in another, the conservationists. In most, all these groups will have a say, sometimes a voluble one.

The key skill for those entrusted with the actual government of cathedrals is to ensure that the interests of the various people who see the place as their own are recognised and balanced, while retaining the Christian mission of the place. This is a crucial task of policy and practice: retaining a clear vision of Christian character and purpose, while enabling a great variety of people to feel that this is home, the kind of home in which there is sustenance, love and renewal. The model is not that of concentric circles, with the cathedral clergy at the centre and casual incomers at the periphery. Rather it is of layers, like an onion, all of which make up the whole. When that is recognised and acted upon, what can become a 'paradisal prison' will in fact be a piece of common ground blessed by God.

TEN

THE SACRED GROVE

Cathedrals and cosmic religion

ANGELA TILBY

I seem to live my life around medieval cathedrals. I have had my home in St Albans for over a decade and for most of that time have been a member of the abbey congregation. I spent nearly six months on sabbatical in the shadow of Durham Cathedral. In my career as a television producer I have made programmes in Lincoln, Canterbury, Salisbury and Wells.

I like these massive monuments, and prefer them to parish churches, because they remain in some important sense both *worldly* and *undomesticated*. It is not just their size that sets them apart – though that is part of it. The basic difference between medieval cathedrals and parish churches is that cathedrals proclaim a form of cosmic religion which still has the power to enchant and scar the imagination, to disturb and exalt the spirit. Along with that, because cathedrals *function* as well as exist, they require a small village of individuals to run them: musicians, craftsmen, vergers, administrators, cleaners, caterers, and salespeople. They are inevitably open to the fluid and changing traffic of the world as it passes by, and comes in and out. If parish churches attract people to the commitment of belonging to a particular praying and worshipping community, cathedrals draw people to drop in without commitment – to wonder and explore. They are a link with the world of leisure, heritage, family outings and tourism.

Cathedrals evoke strong feelings. The plumber who installed my washing machine when I set up home in St Albans, spoke darkly about how he hated the sight of the abbey on the hill, and all it stood for. A former dean had once spoken roughly to someone in his great-grandfather's generation and the insult had never been forgotten. Now the very body of the cathedral stood for the oppression of 'ordinary' people by the clerical establishment. When I visited Lincoln, to make a film with the clinical psychologist Dorothy Rowe, I met individuals who attributed the prevalence of depression in Lincolnshire to some evil influence associated with the cathedral. This was in 1983, long before the more recent troubles. On the other hand, the novelist Susan Howatch has written about the transforming effect of living in sight of Salisbury Cathedral at a point when her life was changing direction; and the columnist Simon Jenkins, not always a friend of the established Church, writes lyrically about the importance of cathedrals in our national life.

When I arrived in Durham for my sabbatical, I found the sheer scale of the building oppressive; wherever I went, it simply *was*; dark and gloomy or golden depending on the time of day. It was a vicious, windy January and the cathedral seemed to be the only object with the strength not to crumple in the gales. Cathedrals do not appear fragile. They have to be strong enough to carry a good deal of human projection. They need to have evil, as well as good aspects; they must be big enough to allow negative as well as positive human feeling to accumulate around themselves. Yet even cathedrals weather and change. I was fascinated to discover that Durham Cathedral's enduring strength was in part illusory. The soft golden sandstone needs specialist treatment so that it is not eroded. Cathedrals crumble without human attention, and the meaning of cathedrals vanishes without our love and fear.

Staying in Canterbury to broadcast an Easter vigil, I was disturbed by the hostility of the regular worshippers who resented the intrusion of a television crew on what for them was the most important night of the year – the only service not usually visited by strangers. I had some sympathy with their distress, though it seems to me now, as it did then, a curious attitude; as though a segment of those who now inhabit the cathedral could imagine that they had the right to close the place down for some purely private function. It was the spirit of congregationalist sectarianism in a setting which seems designed to blow such attitudes away.

❧

In the Middle Ages cathedrals were palaces of light, colour and commerce; sacred and secular jostled together. They represented a continuity between the individual soul, society and the cosmos and their response to God. For us, though, they are simply big, they are spacious, and, except when they are full, they seem to consist of a pillared walkway round a central emptiness. They remind us of a spiritual wholeness we have never had. People don't *rush* inside cathedrals. What one frequently observes in visitors is a leisurely trail around the emptiness, with eyes focused *upwards* on windows and roof bosses, columns and arches. A cathedral is explored by a journey. The whole has to be appropriated by the physical act of walking round the void. The Revd Dr N. T. Wright, dean of Lichfield, told me once that some worshippers and visitors to Lichfield Cathedral found it natural to speak of the cathedral as a 'temple', some going as far as to call it 'the temple of the Lord'. Why is a cathedral more of a temple than a parish church?

The Temple of Christian history and memory is not one among many: it is *the* Temple, the Jewish Temple in Jerusalem. Recent analysis of the texts about the service of the Second

Temple reveals that its existence and rites were seen as having wider significance than for the Jewish community alone.[1] The Temple was a meeting-place between earth and heaven. The worship of the angels was imitated in the Temple service, particularly in the sacrifices of the altar and the role of the high priest, whose vestments expressed the form of the universe. The high priest also wore on his mitre the sacred name through which the cosmos was made. The Zadokite high priest, Simon the Righteous, is reputed to have remarked that the world stands upon three things: the Torah, the Temple service and deeds of loving kindness. Although at least one ancient writer insists on distinguishing the worship of the Temple from that of the sacred groves of paganism,[2] it does seem that the Temple service was a form of cosmic religion, carried out by the Jewish priesthood on behalf of the whole world. Such an understanding of the Temple is carried on into the underside of Christian awareness through the romantic history of the Knights Templar, who lodged, apparently, on the site of Solomon's Temple, while they searched for the Ark of the Covenant.

Like the Temple of Solomon (possibly more splendid in literature than in fact) and Herod's glittering extension of the Second Temple, cathedrals are designed to overwhelm. They give a sense of an order which transcends this world. Cathedrals represent the sacredness of the *one* Temple, transforming the notion of oneness by housing the throne of the one bishop. If cathedrals seem daunting to us – the ever-present reminder of shames and exclusions and insults as well as of delight and awe – how much more daunting they must have seemed in a world without electric light, where most surrounding buildings never reached more than a couple of stories?

But though cathedrals represent oneness, there are, in fact, many of them. Another reason why cathedrals may resemble 'the *Temple*' may be that they represent something of the diversity of ancient, pagan religion. It is striking to a traveller, going up the east coast of England, how cathedrals line the northward journey: Norwich, Ely, Peterborough, Lincoln, York, Durham. The eastern counties of English Christendom are lined with fortresses of faith. It has often been suggested that some of our ancient cathedrals are built on the site of pre-Christian shrines. For those who believe in ley-lines, cathedrals often lie where these 'lines of power' supposedly cross. It was pointed out to me once that Ely Cathedral lies at the centre of a whole cluster of ley-lines. Many cathedrals are also built near wells or springs which had sacred significance in pre-Christian religion. I suppose it is conceivable that there may be some continuous memory of the sacredness of certain places, of a religion more ancient than Christianity associated with them, for which the use of the word 'temple', with its pagan as well as its Jewish overtones, might be a kind of verbal relic.

In support of this speculation Kathleen Basford has drawn attention to the strange phenomenon of carved foliate heads in the stonework of a number of medieval cathedrals, abbeys and parish churches.[3] These bizarre faces, staring out, with vegetation pouring from their mouths, do not have any obvious Christian meaning – yet they are probably the most common decorative theme of the medieval era. They add a touch of unexpected floridity to the most sober screens and doors, roof bosses, tombs, fonts and pillars. The first of the 'green men' Kathleen Basford encountered was at Fountains Abbey. It was a particularly surprising motif in that setting, since the Cistercians who built the abbey shunned most visual decoration and imagery.

Kathleen Basford believes that the origin of foliate heads can be traced back to second-century Roman art. The wreathed male head was a theme both in temple architecture and on triumphal arches, and versions of it are found all over the empire. The leafy head has been described as a 'male Medusa', and there is indeed an example from Mesopotamia in which the head is ringed with serpents. Basford suggests that the foliate head was probably incorporated into church architecture simply as a decorative motif, though she also notes that it is absent in Eastern Christendom. She believes that the figure carried a number of different meanings: it could be read as a celebration of fertility, like the horn of plenty with which it is sometimes associated; or it could take on a more demonic aspect. But the overwhelming link of the green man is with the forest. He streams with foliage. Where better to carve him than in a cathedral, a stone representation of the sacred grove with its tree-like columns, branch-like arches, and play of light from window to aisle, like the dance of the sun's rays across the forest floor? The forest, the sacred grove, is the visual key to what cathedrals represent. Whether intentionally or not, the sculptors and architects saw the forest in the cathedral and the cathedral in the forest. The forest is a symbol of the diversity and complexity of life. It contains growth and decay in constant interrelationship. Life is inconceivable without death, and death is necessary for new life. Whether benign, evil or simply sad (some of the green-man faces appear to be mourning), they eloquently express the unity of creation, the linkage of highest to lowest through the Great Chain of Being.

If this seems absurdly speculative we should remember that the medieval universe was understood as a cosmos in which all beings were related to, and interlinked with, one another. The operative cosmology in the age of the great cathedrals was a blend of biblical storytelling, Aristotelian physics and Ptolemaic astronomy. The act of creation linked the infinite, omnipotent God with both living beings and inanimate objects. Human beings, animals and plants, stars, angels, saints and devils were parts of one grand, hierarchically ordered design of supreme beauty and rationality. Every part bore the imprint of the whole, and thus every part could *symbolise* the whole:

It was not simply that things could be used as symbols, or be invested with symbolic meaning by human beings. They *were* symbols, and the task was to discover their intrinsic significance as such. 'Every created being,' said Honorius of Atun, 'shadows forth truth and life.'[4]

In such an intellectual environment human beings saw themselves as part of the natural order. Nature was endowed with rhythms, and people had no choice but to follow the given pattern of times and seasons in their own lives. It was taken for granted that the heavenly bodies moved round the earth. The geometric patterns of their movements were envisaged as circles of various different kinds and combinations. It was a holistic world. Even numbers were to be seen as divine creatures, each possessing particular qualities and virtues. As Dennis Nineham points out, Augustine had taught that 'the number system is the thoughts of God'.[5] Three was the number of the Trinity, four the number of gospels, winds, and humours. Three and four together made seven, standing for the cardinal virtues, the deadly sins, the number of the sacraments and the gifts of the Holy Spirit. Twelve stood for the tribes of Israel, the apostles and the months of the year.

Numerological analysis was the key to deciphering God's design, not only in nature, but in history. At Chartres, much of the construction, the sculpture and the stained glass are based on numerological motifs. Also at Chartres, as elsewhere, there is plenty of evidence that the zodiac symbols were used for the different months of the year, with all the implications they carry for astrological analysis and prediction. In the age of the great cathedrals it was widely believed that human destiny was influenced by the movements of the heavens. Comets and eclipses were signs of impending disaster. Some church leaders actually practised astrology on behalf of kings and princes.

It is hardly surprising that cathedrals should have been built to express something of the contemporary understanding of the order of the cosmos. In glass and stone, Christ was depicted as the fruit of the Tree of Life – the climax of the generations back to Adam. The rose windows of Chartres announce Jesus' birth into time as the Son of God and the son of Mary, and the Last Judgement at the end of time. Everything is gathered up: time and eternity, human and divine, male and female, sacred and secular.

Medieval cathedrals are a window into a Christianised form of cosmic religion. This is perhaps why they exercise such an appeal. The emotional charge of a medieval cathedral is comparable to that of the Egyptian pyramids or of Stonehenge. All are, in a sense, time-machines. They express a total worldview, inviting onlookers to rediscover their place in the great story of the universe. The extraordinary significance of cathedrals is that they are the only surviving monuments to cosmic religion which still house living communities of prayer and worship.

So it is not surprising that, even today, cathedrals speak to our sense of the wholeness of things: the unity of creation and the place of emerging consciousness within nature. Their sheer scale relativises our individual lives and achievements. The depths of time displayed within them reminds us of our cosmic history. When people visit a cathedral they know that they are in a sacred space which is deeper and older than that of the contemporary Church, and which perhaps fights with the contemporary Church to assert its rather different meaning.

The cathedral viewed as a temple is not a roof and walls that simply enable people to worship: it is itself a place of revelation. The visit *is* the worship. And though it requires staff to administer it and clergy to serve it, it is the building itself which actually mediates presence, strength, reconciliation and consolation.

In the first film of my recent series, *Lives of Jesus,* a deliberate visual parallel was drawn between the life of Wells Cathedral and the Hindu temple of Sri Ranganathaswami near Trichinopoly. This temple contains an image of Vishnu lying on the thousand-headed serpent, and it is known locally, simply as '*the* temple'. To the camera lens there were striking parallels between the activities of the two shrines. Looked at in purely *visual* terms, observing the activities that go on within them, they appear to have more in common with each other than either would have with, say, a parish church.

Both the temple and the cathedral consist of shrines or chapels built around the central point of devotion. In the Hindu temple, this is the image of Vishnu; at Wells, it is the high altar heralded by the magnificent scissor-crossed rood. Both temple and cathedral are designed around space, shade and light, imitating the interplay of space, light and shade in the forest. Both require visitors to make a slow pilgrimage on foot. Both offer visitors the use of light as an aid to prayer: Hindu pilgrims can anoint their faces with the warmth of fire from their hands; Christians can position a votive candle. Both have an abundance of images in stone, wood or plaster, which are used as a focus of devotion and blessing. Both buildings incorporate decorative motifs from the natural world: branches, leaves and animal forms. But above all, both buildings are structured for revelation. Their towers and pillars, their very size, point into the sky, as to the transcendent source of being; yet inside, in the void, all is dark and intimate. The image of Vishnu is within the innermost sanctuary; the rood screen and high altar herald what would have been the central focus of the medieval cathedral: the presence of the sacrament and the relics of the saints. Visitors travel from space to enclosure, from transcendence to immanence, from the cosmic to the personal. Through this pilgrimage they are reminded both of their roots and their destiny. Vishnu rests on the many-headed serpent at Ranganathaswami – an image of divine serenity amid the complexities of creation. At Wells, Christ is stretched on the cross within the arms of the curved strainer arch – an image of the sacrifice which holds the world in being.

One of the most significant parallels between the Hindu temple and the English cathedral is in the presence of money. Both buildings have shops containing devotional objects and aids to prayer. There is an expectation that visitors will part with money; the Hindu temple has a resident elephant to bless those who gave a gift to its keeper. This provides a sense of continuity with normal life; the gap between the sacred and the secular is thin. One is reminded that medieval cathedrals held markets in the nave. Of course for some, the exchange of money for goods in cathedrals is the last straw, evoking the story of Jesus' overthrowing the tables of the money-changers – as though this act had been intended to preclude any commercial activity within the cathedrals of Christendom. Yet the fact that business goes on within the cathedral is a sign that the cathedral offers something which can be paid for: its visitors are not guests, nor are they dependent on the goodwill of their hosts. The legitimate commerce of the modern cathedral, with its bookshops, postcards, refectory, and these days, a turnstile at the door, may give signals that are reassuring rather than excluding for many contemporary visitors. They are not daunted by the possibility of hidden agendas in what is apparently free, but may actually exert pressure to join or give.

Most parish churches, on the other hand, send signals that money is a private matter. There may be boxes for giving; there is a collection in the service; congregations may be encouraged or even pressurised to join stewardship schemes. But this is all very refined and discreet compared with the overt and necessary commercialism of the cathedral – a commercialism with which our contemporaries may well feel at home.

❧

It is often argued that the way in which medieval cathedrals echo pagan and cosmic themes poses a genuine theological problem for contemporary Christianity. Herod's Temple was destroyed at the beginning of the Christian era, never to be rebuilt. Much contemporary scholarship suggests that the genius of early Christianity was in its bold assertion that Christ had, in his own person, replaced the Temple for all time. Where the Temple had offered annual atonement for sins and reconciliation between the human and divine, Christ's sacrifice did away with the necessity of both the sacrificial system and the mediating role of the Temple priesthood. The destruction of the Temple in the early Christian era was hugely significant: it marked the birth of both Christianity and rabbinic Judaism as separate and competing faiths. No longer could any mere building be regarded as a container for revelation. Language about the Temple is spiritualised both in Paul and the rabbis. In Christianity it is worshippers of Jesus who are now to embody the life of the Temple. In Judaism, the home becomes a small-scale temple, the laws of purity are transferred from the altar to the kitchen. Churches and synagogues are to have no sacred status – they are merely meeting places.

If this argument is upheld, the cosmic religion of medieval cathedrals can only be seen as an aberration, a deep misunderstanding of the heart of the Christian Gospel. This critique would not only be held by those who might want to argue that the errors of medievalism were challenged and corrected by the teachings of the Reformation; much contemporary Catholic teaching is equally critical of 'cosmic' religion. Yet the cosmic religion of the cathedrals remains and is, as I have argued, one of the main reasons for their appeal. In an age of global culture and ecological concern, there are many who find that the tight, club-like communities of parish churches ask for too much commitment and arouse too much anxiety. Parish life cannot easily feed the spiritual need to locate oneself in the wider cosmos; it has no language for the impersonal aspects of the godward journey; it does not naturally display the integration of aspects of nature into sacred history. It offers no obvious models for the slow journey from a sense of transcendence to a recovery of intimacy with oneself and the world.

Cathedrals today display an ambivalence towards their spiritual past. There is little evidence that cosmic religion is valued, or even understood; rather, a conscious effort is made to promote cathedrals in terms of their *function*. They are, for example, very big and attractive buildings which enhance the communities in which they are set. They are a setting for concerts, exhibitions, drama festivals, *son et lumière* displays. They are also the mother churches of their dioceses and seats of the bishops. They are the focuses of communities of prayer and teaching. They have important musical traditions and promote excellence in public worship. All this is obvious, and needs to be said – and yet it does not really grapple with the problem cathedrals pose for the Church, nor with their potential.

The unsimple fact is that the message of *usefulness* is at war with the more immediate message of sheer presence and power. Cathedrals are very big, mysterious buildings. The flimsy exhibition boards with mug-shots of the staff and clergy look rather quaint compared with the brooding carvings of saints and apostles. One suspects that the understandable attempt to communicate the presence of a living community in the cathedral is not of interest to those who visit. What is much more obvious to them is the impersonality of the place. This is one Christian place of prayer where you are unlikely to be stopped or questioned or even noticed. Your presence is taken for granted, but nobody attempts to name or categorise you.

The messages delivered on hoardings about mission or human rights seem at odds with the building's containment of both good and evil in its representation of the cosmic design. Cathedrals are place of awe, not morality. Their architecture does not judge or arbitrate. The devils and demons, gargoyles and sad green men, have their place here along with the angels and saints. In contrast, the earnest displays of what the Church is doing to improve life in the community may make those who live, work and worship in the cathedral feel more comfortable – but they are contradicted by a mere sweep of the eye. The cathedral visitor may know that the world is a rough and ready place; the cathedral sets the sins and hopes of humanity within a cosmic framework in which there is no expectation that affairs of the realm, or the wars of nations, or the petty injustices of life, will get much better.

It is the historical rupture at the birth of Christianity which lies behind our ambivalence towards cathedrals. We are unsure about the legitimacy of cosmic religion, just as we are unsure about the theology and the spirituality of medieval Christianity. Dennis Nineham's terrifying portrait of the early medieval world makes much of the discomfort and cruelty of the era: its closeness to paganism, its superstition and barbarity, and its overwhelming sense of God as inexorable and distant Judge. Yet the cathedral itself is a witness to the beauty and vision which could grow from such unpromising roots. Perhaps we need to decipher cathedrals as containers for the struggle between prophetic and cosmic faith. The historical events of the life of Christ are here set within a slow and measured timescale. There is no resolution of the tension in the structure of the cathedral – only the lasting strength of what is achieved by the holding together of opposites. It is arguable that modern Christianity overemphasises the prophetic and ethical dimensions of faith, and it is left to cathedrals to right the balance. It is important that they are allowed to do so. After all, it is the very terrors of barbarism and judgement which inform the spiritual issues of our own era. We are daily aware of the effects of human cruelty, corruption and false belief. As we face the threat of ecological meltdown, there is huge anxiety about the judgement which might await the human race. Modern

Christianity seems able only to stress the nearness and intimacy of God, having shunned any realistic account of both hell and the demons. But it is increasingly recognised that, without a doctrine of creation that addresses contemporary cosmology, Christian proclamation seems timid and feeble – its attempts to be prophetic no more than superficial moralising.

The cathedral challenges us with the possibility that modern Christianity does not really understand the potential richness of the treasures it guards. If it did, would there not be more of an attempt to integrate holistic themes into contemporary artworks commissioned by cathedrals? Would there not be more of an attempt to build bridges with the worlds of science, technology and communication which increasingly hold the key of knowledge and power in today's community? There is, I believe, a hunger for cosmic religion which the Churches are unwilling and unable to meet. This is, in the first place, because there is a loss of confidence in the resources of theology to interpret the picture of our world which is emerging from science. Following from this, the Churches have defined their contribution to society in terms of good causes: Churches are too often reduced to being humanistic ethical clubs, lacking the imaginative vision of the wholeness of things for which people crave.

～～✣～～

What would cosmic religion look like if it were to be taken seriously by today's cathedrals? One answer is to look at what has been offered over the last two decades by the annual festival of Mind, Body and Spirit in London. This is a marketplace of spiritualities, philosophies and therapies, and also a gathering place for a wide network of those who want to explore different traditions of wisdom without going too far from home. Cathedrals could offer smaller, localised versions of the festival, opening the doors to insights from the old and new faiths and spiritualities in our midst. This need not imply either acceptance or criticism of such wisdom traditions, merely the fact that the cathedral is uniquely able to bring them under its roof. An area could be set aside to fulfil the role of the Temple as 'a house of prayer for all nations', which drew on the symbols and Scriptures of non-Christian faiths. One example of a Christian community which has explored the hosting of a wide variety of alternatives, yet without losing its prophetic Christian edge, is St James's, Piccadilly.

Cathedrals could go further in exploring cosmic religion by commissioning works which make religious play of what we now know of the world of nature: the streaming forth of energy from the primal simplicity of the big bang; the four fundamental forces, the diversity of life on earth, the energies of the atom and the delicate, fleeting existence of subatomic particles, the twining and replicating of the double helix. This is the cosmological background which science has revealed to us, and the great interpretative challenge for the Christian artist or theologian is to set the story of creation, fall and redemption through the cross of Christ within the cosmology that the vast majority of people now accept as authoritative.

This is a hugely difficult task. The enterprise of science effectively disconnected itself from both our humanistic and spiritual traditions at the Enlightenment. But now it is widely acknowledged that the decoupling of science and spirituality has left us bereft; we have orphaned ourselves, losing our sense of rootedness in the universe. It is this rootedness and belonging that people seek in religious experience, but so often they are fobbed off by the kind of domesticated religion that does not expect any more than loyalty and good behaviour, denying both their worldliness and their capacity for sacrifice.

We could begin by interpreting what we already have – not just aesthetically, but theologically – to explore the linkages of the medieval world in ways which open up our own connectedness. To set the Christian vision within a modernised version of the framework already offered by our cathedrals would be to honour the toil of generations of craftsmen, designers and artists, and to ensure that cathedrals are not only houses of the dead, but sanctuaries for the living and the unborn.

ELEVEN

SETTING A COURSE

Cathedrals and the future

STEPHEN PLATTEN AND CHRISTOPHER LEWIS

In which direction ought cathedrals to steer themselves as they look to the future? On what model of the Church should they draw, and what are the sources of such a model? The approach taken in this book, as we have attempted to answer these questions, has been deliberately multifaceted. The method has not been purely historical nor uniquely theological. Aspects of each of these disciplines, and of many others, have been pressed into service in an attempt to understand better both the role and intellectual rationale for cathedrals in our contemporary world. As these flagships steer a course across the oceans of human experience and encounter, so it is helpful to use a great variety of different instruments to chart positions and plot suitable patterns for the future voyage. Radar and computer stand alongside compass and sextant; descriptions of the crew and of the construction of the superstructure are related to the rhythms of life and the traditions of marine navigation. What have these varied reflections to teach us?

As we have distilled conclusions from these reflections, it has become clear that there is a uniqueness about people's perceptions and expectations of cathedrals. These perceptions are understandably different from their feelings about great secular buildings, but they also differ, to a large extent, from their response to other churches. Susan Hill reflects: 'People do not come to the cathedral because it is the same as other places, but because it is not'.[1] Throughout the different essays are phrases echoing similar instincts: 'They touch an emotional nerve . . . They draw people in through their music . . . They may be beacons for our nation . . . Like an onion with many layers they offer something at different levels for a whole host of humanity'. Even a strictly theological reflection upon 'a cathedral as the bishop's church' reveals that these buildings have a distinctive role. It is a public role which opens up to people aspects of a universal realm of meaning expressed through our common humanity, and particularly through a common religious experience. They are potentially, as another writer puts it, places where we may encounter 'cosmic religion'. This description of the theological and ecclesiological role of cathedrals may have a longer historical pedigree than we realise.

In analysing the history of the English Church in the nineteenth century, Owen Chadwick makes it clear that puzzlement about the precise role of cathedrals is no new phenomenon. He writes of the early nineteenth century in particular:

> No one knew what cathedrals were for. By the beauty of their music and singing they set forth the glory of God; and yet it was confessed that if the choirs of Durham and Canterbury were models of decorum and of art, the choirs of some cathedrals . . . were renowned for slipshod irreverence.[2]

As the century wore on, so more and more thought was put into the reform of the cathedrals, and into discovering precisely what might be the rationale for their existence. With the religious revival of the mid nineteenth century, preaching assumed a new prominence in the Church as a whole, but it was still not clear that this would help the cathedrals: 'The cathedral lost place as England became industrial'.[3] Preaching was not universally going to offer the answer, but instead the openness of these great churches to a public role began once again to emerge:

> Thus the great cathedrals were not able to do what Spurgeon could do [i.e. they were not able to adapt themselves to become great 'preaching boxes', and thus attract vast crowds as Spurgeon had been able to do]. And yet they were more slowly finding a pastoral opportunity of a different kind, more suitable to their genius. They endeavoured to reach outward.[4]

Certainly that was the direction in which cathedrals would move. The final denouement of that process would have to wait until the first part of the twentieth century, with the work of Dean Bennett and others – but the course had been set with reforms to the cathedrals in the nineteenth century. Other more recent developments have further reinforced that particular sense of direction, including specifically the vast growth of tourism as an industry. Huge numbers of people now visit cathedrals for undeniably non-religious reasons, but in the process may sometimes be moved by their encounter with these great tracts of enclosed sacred space. Alongside this, however, something has emerged at a deeper level, which has been alluded to in these different essays. There has been a growing sense that cathedrals as institutions are capable of echoing the fears and aspirations, the needs and the accomplishments, of contemporary society. They can even act as mirrors to the nation, or to a particular local community or region, in a great variety of different ways. This may be may be most obvious at times of great crisis or celebration, but it remains as a potential resource throughout more mundane periods within the life of the nation.

Economic and cultural development may offer us one example. Some regions of Britain have suffered more sharply than others during the past 30 years, through the radical economic and industrial revolutions that we have experienced. Cathedrals have sometimes been able to focus and reflect these concerns for the wider community – for example, the reactions to the miners' strike in 1984. But this role is not restricted to cathedrals set within larger industrial conurbations: cathedrals set at the heart of rural areas can also focus the aspirations and fears of the local community and region. More specifically, moments of crisis can identify a similar role for cathedrals. The Hillsborough football disaster in 1989 was a classic example of this. Sheffield Cathedral, and both the Roman Catholic and Anglican cathedrals in Liverpool, played a most significant part in helping the two cities to articulate their grief, and to set it within the context of what one might loosely call 'contemporary spirituality'. Given that cathedrals do perform such a role, what part does it play within a wider theology of the Church? One way forward might be to imagine a variety of different future scenarios.

Picture a city centre with its shops and offices, houses or blocks of flats. People mill around and go about their business. Some conform more or less to the image of that rather elusive being, the modern secular person: they live and work largely without reference to God – or indeed to anyone or anything transcendent. They may say the occasional prayer, go to a wedding here or a funeral there, even be drawn to light a candle and attach to it some intention or hope. But their beliefs and behaviour are mainly secular. Others, however, may go further and be religious. For a number that will mean active participation in a religious group – yet for many their behaviour is best described as 'believing without belonging'. In other words, they have religious beliefs but do not see that their beliefs imply membership of a religious gathering.

It is misleading to speak as if people were either committed or uncommitted, religious or non-religious. Numerous studies have shown that human beings are not like that, for their religious attitudes and behaviour may vary at different times and places: the 'orthodox' rarely conform to religious stereotypes, whereas 'unbelievers' have rich and varied ways of making sense of reality. In the past (whenever that was!), the degree of conformity was probably far less than is supposed. Now, in the West, the pluralism which has been a feature of every age is public and indeed celebrated.

So this city will contain a great mixture of all kinds of people whose beliefs and behaviour will be hard to predict. And it will contain numerous models of religious activity, in mosques and chapels, regular meetings and occasional events. Let us focus on three models which may be of particular significance for the future.

The first is a gathered community of committed Christian believers. In this city they meet in a school hall and consist, on the whole, of young and quite successful people. Membership of the group is clearly defined, and that definition is not only a matter of holding particular beliefs but also of financial commitment, frequent social interaction and shared religious experience. The church (which outsiders might define as a sect) is set apart from other religious groups, both those which call themselves Christian and those of other faiths. It plays a negligible part in ecumenical (and certainly in inter-faith) endeavours. Many see such a committed and exclusive group as the desirable, or at least inevitable, Christian pattern for the future – and in a fragmented society, it does provide certainty and security. In numerical terms, it is a success.

Now let us focus on a contrasting group, which may also be hailed as appropriate for the future. To call it a group is perhaps an exaggeration, for it is more of a loose association of people with a similar longing for peace and self-discovery. They meet in the city above a shop which sells New Age literature, dream catchers and crystals. Their beliefs are in the area of natural healing, psychic peace and generally being in tune with the natural world – a world of mystery, populated by spiritual beings. Their cathedrals are within, or perhaps arboreal, or at Glastonbury. There is something in common with Christianity and some of this overlap is explicit, for example in the group's endorsement of selected aspects of 'Celtic' spirituality. Yet the individuals are focused not on the person of Jesus, on service of the poor, or on evangelism, but rather on individual transformation: a personal journey along a benign route to self-fulfilment.

Out of the many possible models, now let us envisage a third. The city is a northern one and at its centre is a cathedral, not at all Barchester-like, for it is a former parish church full of signs of industrial civic pride. What might its role be, and how does it relate to the other two ways of being religious described above? It has a regular Anglican congregation with expectations much like those of numerous parish churches. The members share some of the beliefs of the sect and also some of those of the spiritual association, but the context is very different. Part of this context is set by the actual building, central and accessible – but part is also set by people, for the congregation and its clergy are by no means the only ones who see it as their cathedral. Congregationalism is not an option, for who can say to whom the cathedral really belongs? Bishop and diocese, county and city, volunteers and visitors – all have a claim. They are not all Christian believers in the orthodox sense, for some with an interest in the cathedral may be very secular and some may belong to other faiths. Yet here is an explicitly Christian place, marked by Christian worship and activity, to which all may come and which may (if it does its job properly) express many of the hopes and fears of those who live in the city and beyond, and may also challenge them.

The implications of the different contributions within this book is that cathedrals offer a particular ecclesiological model for the future. It is not the only model available, as we have just agreed – but it is a model that is capable of holding together a broad range of concerns on behalf of wider society, and interpreting these in the light of a universal framework of meaning. Evidence for this contention is adduced from the way in which people are drawn to cathedrals at times of crisis. We have already noted, in the Hillsborough tragedy, one such case on the local level; many other less dramatic examples could be cited.

But on other occasions the crisis may be national, with the cathedrals still playing a seminal part in the life of the city or region within which they are set. In 1997, this was seen most dramatically in the extraordinary outpouring of emotion and seeking after some form of spiritual solace, in the days that followed the death of Diana, Princess of Wales. This event hit the world somewhat in the manner of the death of President John Kennedy a generation earlier. In the intervening period, however, formal religion in Britain had become still more marginal to people's lives. Furthermore, the increased professionalism and effectiveness of the media helped heighten the public consciousness of loss and the need to grieve. The Princess' death and its sequel were international in their effects and reverberations, but understandably it was in England where these emotions were most acutely felt. There was no part of the community left unaffected, and civic as well as ecclesiastical strands within society were all engaged by the experience – city halls and even county offices were caught up in the nation's response, as people sought some means of expressing their emotions.

Cathedrals played a prominent and distinctive part in the response: all of them found themselves daily adapting to the public expression of grief and loss. Initially the response was at the level of receiving flowers and making available books of condolence. It soon became apparent, however, that the general public – including very large numbers who had no formal church connection – were seeking other and deeper means of expressing their need for some spiritual comfort and response. The precise approach adopted by individual cathedrals varied greatly. Some held memorial services during the week following the Princess' death, while others set up vigils the night before the funeral. Still others opted for a service on the day of the funeral itself. The liturgies sought to offer something that resonated with a wider public, using prayers and hymns that might be familiar even to the unchurched. The lighting of candles, which has become so popular for tourists and pilgrims in cathedrals, proliferated and often formed the centrepiece for a vigil or a service of thanksgiving for the Princess' life. The enhanced role of the media intersected on this occasion with the role of cathedrals, and the government used television to transmit the funeral service itself to a number of cathedrals, allowing people throughout the country a degree of participation in the service. The cathedrals thus acted as regional focuses – indeed, people of different religions found them to be places where they could satisfy their spiritual needs.

Seen through such experiences, then, the cathedral model is Christian and yet inclusive. While retaining its Christian commitment, the cathedral offers occasions when those of other faiths can come to pray. Many other churches (Anglican, Roman Catholic, Free Church) may also work to this pattern – but we are suggesting here that the future of cathedrals lies in a particular way of being the Church, and that the future of the Church is informed by the ecclesiology, lived out in cathedrals. Religious success in our culture may indeed lie with the sect or with the spiritual association, and in that sense the role of the cathedral is countercultural; but there remains a crucial place for some churches plainly and publicly to model another way of being religious and of being Christian.

The distinctiveness of this cathedral ecclesiology is not dependent on great size, age or beauty. It is dependent on a cathedral being a special, open, transcendent building which is the bishop's seat, and on its having obligations which force the life of the place to be outward-looking, even when the pressures of the age encourage religious (and secular) introversion. The best guide is a careful use of the theology of incarnation – avoiding the static, structural sense derived from the image of 'the body of Christ', and emphasising instead Christian interrelatedness and commitment to context. For incarnation can be understood in the dynamic sense of involving dedicated service to people and to place. So it is proper for cathedrals to be concerned day by day with the issues that matter to a particular community, be they poverty, homelessness or urban regeneration. Incarnation demands an active presence, and should not exclude a prophetic stance when that is appropriate.

A cathedral is not only a place to which people come. It is also a place through which they go, and from which they emerge renewed. It is a place of interaction, between people and with God: not in order to escape from the world around, but rather to renew commitment to it. That is true for the local person who comes for a special occasion and leaves with new resolve, for example to do voluntary work in the community. It is also true of the visitors who make a point of saying where they are from, thus being able to see themselves both as representatives of their own church and as part of the wider Church, and returning home with new insight. And it is true of the person who is seeking and is then converted to faith in Jesus Christ.

Cathedrals are not everything and are not for everyone. There is a passage in D. H. Lawrence's *The Rainbow* where a couple, having reacted very differently to the great cathedral at Lincoln, realise that it is not all-embracing:

> He listened to the thrushes in the garden and heard a note which the cathedrals did not include: something free and careless and joyous. He crossed a field that was all yellow with dandelions, on his way to work, and the bath of yellow glowing was something at once so sumptuous

and so fresh, that he was glad he was away from the shadowy cathedral.[5]

From the beginning of the last century, there has been intermittent debate about what cathedrals are for. There have been numerous answers: for learning, for experiencing heritage, for the diocese, for reconciliation, as places of refuge and prayer. The contention here is that their main role is to demonstrate and live a crucial way of being the Church. Cathedrals are places which struggle to point both to the eternal and to the temporal, in an age when that is an almost impossible task. So they are models of what the Church can be: flagships of the spirit.

NOTES AND REFERENCES

INTRODUCTION

1. Quoted in Roger Lloyd, *The Church of England 1900–1965*, (London, SCM Press, 1966), p. 387.
2. op. cit., p. 387.
3. op. cit., p. 396.

1. AT THE STILL POINT OF THE TURNING WORLD
Susan Hill

The title of this essay is taken from *The Four Quartets* by T. S. Eliot.
Susan Hill's novels include: *In the Springtime of the Year, Strange Meeting, I'm the King of the Castle, The Woman In Black, Air and Angels*. She has also written two autobiographical books, *The Magic Apple Tree* and *Family*, and a number of children's books and collections of short stories.

2. FRIENDS OF ALBION?
Christopher Rowland

1. *Jerusalem* 40:3; 48:27 and especially 71:13–14:
   their Villages, Towns, Cities, Sea-Ports, Temples, sublime Cathedrals,
   All were his Friends.
2. W. Benjamin, 'Theses on the Philosophy of History' in *Illuminations* (London, Fontana, 1978), p. 248 (Thesis 7): '[Cultural treasures] owe their existence not only to the efforts of the great minds and talents who created them but also to the anonymous toil of their contemporaries. There is no document of civilisation which is not at the same time a document of barbarism.'

3. *Heritage and Renewal*, The Report of the Archbishops' Commission on Cathedrals (London, Church House Publishing, 1994), p. 190. One of the curious features about this report is the absence of any theological rationale.

4. Bede, 'De Templo', in *Translated Texts for Historians* (Liverpool, Liverpool University Press, 1995).

5. Minucius Felix Octav. 32.

6. See C. Myers, *Binding the Strong Man* (Maryknoll, New York, Orbis, 1989), p. 364.

7. Heb. 13:13; Exod. 33:7; Lev. 24:16; Num. 15; 35. See also M. Isaacs, *Sacred Space: An Approach to the Theology of the Epistle to the Hebrews* (Sheffield, Sheffield Academic Press, 1992).

8. K. Barth 'Biblical questions: insights and vistas' in *The Word of God and the Word of Man*, (London, Hodder & Stoughton, 1976), p. 474.

9. See P. G. Cobb, 'The architectural setting of the liturgy', in C. Jones, G. Wainwright, E. Yarnold & P. Bradshaw, *The Study of Liturgy* (London, SPCK, 1992), p. 528.

10. See A. Kreider, *Worship and Evangelism in Pre-Christendom* (Nottingham, Grove Books, 1995).

11. On the ways in which the passage about the anointing at Bethany is used by contemporary British Christians, see *The Gospel, the Poor and the Churches* (Christian Aid, May 1994).

12. Blake, *Milton* 40:22f ('religion hid in war named moral virtue'), and *Jerusalem* 75:20.

13. *Heritage and Renewal*, p. 45.

14. Susan White, 'Theology and sacred space' in D. Brown & A. Loades, *The Sense of the Sacramental* (London, SPCK, 1995), p. 42f.

15. Blake, *Jerusalem* 48:14.

3. CATHEDRALS AND THEIR COMMUNITIES
Nicolas Alldrit

1. Acts 2:4ff; 4:32ff.

2. Bede, *Ecclesiastical History* i.27.

3. Gervase of Canterbury, as quoted in C. H. Lawrence, *Mediaeval Monasticism* (London, 1984), p. 122.

4. Quoted in M. Deanesly, *A History of the Mediaeval Church* (London, 1973).

5. *If Nothing Hinders* (Lincoln, 1983), p. 9.

6. John 13:16–38; 14:1–31.

7. Eth.Nic. 9.8.2. 1168b.

8. Esther de Waal, *Seeking God: The Way of St Benedict* (London, Collins, 1984).

4. WALKING IN PATTERNS
David Stancliffe

1. Avery Dulles, *Models of the Church* (Dublin, Gill and Macmillan, 1976).
2. David Stancliffe, 'Creating sacred space: liturgy and architecture', in *The Sense of the Sacramental*, David Brown and Ann Loades (eds) (SPCK, London, 1995).
3. See Christopher Wordsworth, 'The introduction to the Sarum Processionale', in *Ceremonies and Processions of the Cathedral Church of Salisbury* (Cambridge, Cambridge University Press, 1901).
4. These narrative readings are drawn in part from the Armenian lectionary: see John Wilkinson, *Egeria's Travels*, Note E, pp. 253–77, (London, SPCK, 1971).
5. See Paul Bradshaw, *Two Ways of Praying* (London, SPCK, 1995), Chapter 1. On the history and development of the daily office generally, see George Guiver, *Company of Voices* (London, SPCK, 1988).
6. *The Care of Cathedrals Measure*, Clause 1.
7. Lumen Gentium, *Constitution on the Church*, Article 1, Documents of the Second Vatican Council.
8. See *Eucharistic Presidency* – a theological statement by the House of Bishops of the Church of England, GS1248, sections 4.47–4.51; and *The Liturgical Ministry of Deacons* – a report by the Church of England Liturgical Commission, GS Misc.281 *passim*.

5. MUSIC IN THESE STONES
Richard Shephard

1. *Us and our Song School*
2. Bede, *History of the English Church and People* (Harmondsworth, Penguin 1968).
3. S. S. Wesley, *A Few Words on Cathedral Music* (1849).
4. ibid.
5. ibid.
6. ibid.
7. Choir Schools' Association Annual Census.
8. Much confusion exists about the term 'choir school'. In this country there is only one school, Westminster Abbey, which educates only chor-

isters. In all other choir schools, the choristers form a varying percentage of the pupils.

9. Dora Robertson, *Sarum Close* p. 152.
10. S. S. Wesley, *A Few Words on Cathedral Music*, p. 57.
11. *In Tune With Heaven*, p. 256.
12. *Heritage and Renewal*, p. 178.
13. Jonathan Harvey, *Contemporary Church Music* (Friends of Cathedral Music Report, 1987).
14. William Mathias, *Composing for the Church* (FCM Report, 1987).
15. Peter Shaffer, *Amadeus* Act II, p. 105.
16. Philip Titcombe, *Some Reflections on the Music of York Minster* (1991).
17. Kenneth Grahame, *The Wind in the Willows*, Chapter 1.
18. *Heritage and Renewal*.
19. See Kenneth Long, *The Music of the English Church* (1971), p. 38.

6. BUILDING AND CHERISHING
Andrew Anderson

1. *The Times* 24 August 1992.
2. David L. Edwards, *The Cathedrals of Britain* (Andover, Pitkin Pictorials, 1989); Christopher Wilson, *The Gothic Cathedral* (London, Thames and Hudson, 1990).
3. John Harvey, *English Medieval Architects* (Gloucester, Alan Sutton Publishing, 1984).
4. Wilson, *The Gothic Cathedral*.
5. Jaques Heyman, *The Stone Skeleton* (Cambridge, Cambridge University Press, 1995).
6. Bruckner, *Three Graduals for the Church Year for Mixed Voices* (New York, USA. C. F. Peters Corporation, 1961).
7. Morris West, *The Devil's Advocate* (London, Heinemann, 1959).
8. British Standards Institute, *Guide to the Principles of the Conservation of Historic Buildings* (in draft January 1998).
9. Cathedrals Fabric Commission for England and the Care of Cathedrals Measure (1990): *An Explanatory Note* issued by the CFCE (undated).
10. Morris West, *Daughter of Silence* (London, Heinemann, 1961).

7. JEWELS IN THE DUST
Keith Walker

1. Aldous Huxley, *The Perennial Philosophy* (London, Chatto & Windus, 1946), p. 342.
2. Keith Walker, *Images or Idols* (Norwich, Canterbury Press 1996), pp. 96–105.
3. W. R. Inge, *God and the Astronomers* (Harlow, Longman Green 1933), p. 192; see also P. Roubiczek, *Ethical Values in the Age of Science* (Cambridge, Cambridge University Press, 1969), pp. 250–3, 267–94, etc.
4. Philip Sherrard, *The Sacred in Art and Life* (Golgonooza Press, 1990), p. 82.
5. S. T. Coleridge, *Biographia Litereria* (Nonesuch Press, 1933), Vol. 1, ch. xiii.
6. Walker, *Images or Idols*, pp. 82–96.
7. Author's archive.
8. Author's archive.
9. Inge, *God and the Astronomers*, p. 202.

8. LOCUS ISTE
Stephen Platten

1. cf. the words of Anton Bruckner's anthem, popular in cathedral musical repertoires: 'Locus iste a Deo factus est, inaestimabile sacramentum, irreprehensibilis est'. ('This place was made by God a priceless mystery; it is without reproof.')
2. *The Diary of the Reverend Francis Kilvert: Selections* (London, Jonathan Cape, 1944, 1978), p. 97 (Wednesday, 21 December 1870).
3. Peter Brown, *The Cult of the Saints* (London, SCM Press, 1981), p. 86.
4. op. cit., pp. 40–41.
5. cf. J. Ninian Comper, *Of the Christian Altar and the Buildings which Contain It* (London, SPCK, 1950), pp. 8, 9.
6. *Baptism, Eucharist and Ministry* (Geneva, World Council of Churches, 1982), p. 27.
7. Robert Runcie, *One in Hope* (London, CTS/SPCK, 1989), p. 21.
8. Encyclical Letter, *Ut Unum Sint* (Vatican City, 25 May 1995).
9. Robert Taft, *The Liturgy of the Hours in the East and West* (Collegeville, The Liturgical Press, 1986), p. 55.
10. op cit. pp. 141–164.
11. George Guiver CR, *Company of Voices* (London, SPCK, 1988), p. 96.
12. Wesley Carr (ed.), *Say One For Me* (London, SPCK, 1992), pp. 63–71.

13. cf. David Lodge's novels: *Paradise News* (Harmondsworth, Penguin, 1991); *Therapy* (Harmondsworth, Penguin, 1995).

9. HUMAN EBB AND FLOW
Christopher Lewis

1. 'The Bishop's Charge' (Diocese of Salisbury, 1991), p. 26.
2. Jean Gimpel, *The Cathedral Builders* (Salisbury, Michael Russell, 1983), e.g. p. 6.
3. F. S. M. Bennett, *The Nature of a Cathedral* (London, Mowbray, 1925), p. 6.
4. John Shirley (ed.), *The Reminiscences of the Reverend George Gilbert* (Canterbury, Canterbury Cathedral, 1938), pp. 14–15.
5. Oliver Fiennes, *Bad Dreams and Bright Visions* (Lincoln, Lincoln Cathedral, 1988), p. 2.
6. Henry Jenkyns, *The Remains of Thomas Cranmer* (Oxford, Oxford University Press, 1833), Vol. I, p. 292 (letter written to Thomas Cromwell on 29 November 1539).
7. Christopher Lewis, 'Cathedrals: restricting and liberating space', *Theology*, Vol. XCVIII (1988), pp. 179–86.
8. The opening words of L. P. Hartley's novel, *The Go-Between* (London, Hamish Hamilton, 1954), p. 1.
9. David Lowenthal, *The Past is a Foreign Country* (Cambridge, Cambridge University Press, 1985), p. 296.
10. E. W. Benson, *The Cathedral* (London, John Murray, 1878), p. 43.

10. THE SACRED GROVE
Angela Tilby

1. Such as the study by C. T. R. Hayward, *The Jewish Temple* (London, Routledge, 1996).
2. Hectaeus of Abdera, as quoted in Hawyard, *The Jewish Temple*, p. 20.
3. Kathleen Basford, *The Green Man* (Ipswich, D. S. Brewer, 1978).
4. Dennis Nineham, *Christianity Mediaeval and Modern* (London, SCM, 1993), p. 22.
5. Nineham, *Christianity Mediaeval and Modern*, p. 25.

11. SETTING A COURSE
Stephen Platten and Christopher Lewis

1. See p. 15.
2. Owen Chadwick, *The Victorian Church* (London, 1966), Part I, p. 140.
3. op. cit., p. 523.
4. op. cit., p. 526.
5. D. H. Lawrence, *The Rainbow* (Harmondsworth, Penguin, new edition, 1971), p. 206.

INDEX

❦